MW00334684

Living with a Functioning Alcoholic

A Woman's Survival Guide

Neill Neill, Ph.D.
Registered Psychologist
Diplomate, Comprehensive Energy
Psychology

Living with a Functioning Alcoholic
A Woman's Survival Guide

Copyright © 2008 by Neill Neill. All rights reserved. The contents of this book may not be reproduced by any means in whole or in part without the written permission of the author.

ISBN: 978-0-9810843-0-5

Contact Information

Dr. Neill Neill
235 Crescent Road West
Qualicum Beach
British Columbia
Canada V9K 1J9

(250)752-8684
DrNeill@neillneill.com
www.neillneill.com
www.alcoholism.neillneill.com

Cover design by Cailin Green, www.cailingreen.com

Neill Neill Press

Dedication

This book is dedicated with love to the memory of

my youngest brother Richard, who ended his life to escape troubling mental problems in the aftermath of earlier drug abuse,

my son Richard, who died of liver disease and cancer more than a decade after he overcame his alcohol addiction,

and

my son Colin, who died of heart failure, a complication of the alcohol and drug addiction he fought so bravely.

How to Get the Most out of this Book

Congratulations! You are embarking on a journey of personal change. I have six suggestions for you to get the most out of your reading.

1.   If you have not already done so, get my free mini-ebook, **addiction and Codependency Simplified** at www.alcoholism.neillneill.com/codependecy/. You will receive occasional notices of future updates, new articles, teleseminars, recordings and things I haven't even thought of yet.

2.   Keep a notebook and pen nearby as you read each chapter so you can make notes when you need to. At the end of each Chapter, there is at least one question to reflect on before you read on. Each starts with the word "Reflection." Use your notebook. Writing is the doing part of thinking.

3.   Read Part One first. The three short chapters will give you a good overview of the book and why I wrote it for you.

4.   If you have not already taken my "Alcoholism Test for the Alcoholic Marriage" at www.alcoholism.neillneill.com/alcoholism-test/, it is reprinted at the back of this book as an appendix. Check it out.

5.   If there is any possibility you or your children are unsafe in your relationship, read Chapter 24 right away.

6.   Although I make many recommendations in the pages of this book, what I say is informational and educational in nature. It is not therapy. You alone are responsible for how you understand and use what I say.

If you need specific advice or therapy, this book is not a substitute for appropriate professional assistance. If you are already receiving professional help, do by all means use the contents of this book to get the most out of that professional relationship.

Dr. Neill Neill

Living with a Functioning Alcoholic

A Woman's Survival Guide

Neill Neill, Ph.D.

Part One
Introduction: It's about Much More than Survival

Chapter 1
A Book Addressed to You Instead of Your Alcoholic Partner

If you are a woman in a relationship, and your partner is or has been abusing alcohol, *Living with a Functioning Alcoholic* is addressed to you. Life with a problem drinker poses many special challenges, both in understanding and then in taking action.

Note: *Living with a Functioning Alcoholic* uses the terms "partner," "boyfriend" and "spouse" more or less interchangeably. The manual is written from the point of view that you are in a relationship with someone.

However, *Living with a Functioning Alcoholic* is still addressed to you if you have left a relationship with a problem drinker and are now trying to make sense of your life. You will find help in regaining your courage to consider a new relationship, should you want to. You will find guidance in avoiding a repetition of the old patterns and going through all the heartache again.

Living with a Functioning Alcoholic is addressed to you, because it is usually the woman who takes the trouble to do the research to try to understand a family problem. It is usually the woman who first seeks professional help with an alcohol abuse problem in the family. ·

Make no mistake about it: alcohol abuse is a family issue.

Your legacy to your children and grandchildren is not the toys you give them. Instead, they will remember how well you lived your life, physically, emotionally and spiritually. Your greatest gift to your family is your good example.

Good Information Falls By the Wayside

There is a great deal of information available to alcohol users who suspect they are developing an alcohol problem. Many books are addressed to alcoholics.

Such books are sometimes helpful to recovering alcoholics trying to understand where they have come from and how to improve their lives. Such books may help recovering alcoholics understand why it seems to be taking years for them to get back to "normal" after they have survived the acute withdrawal phase of recovery.

My experience with functioning alcoholics, unfortunately, is they typically don't read books, at least not books about alcoholism. They are too much in denial. And therefore most of this good information falls by the wayside.

There are many books addressed to alcoholics, who don't read them, but there are very few resources addressed specifically to the women living with partners who abuse alcohol. And it's the women who do read.

An Ocean of Misinformation

To make matters worse, there is a great deal of mis-information out there about alcohol abuse and alcoholism. There is controversy even about what alcoholism is. There is controversy about what causes it. There is controversy about treatment.

If you are starting to worry that your partner may have a drinking problem, you need to arm yourself with some solid information about problem drinking and alcoholism.

You need to be aware of some claims that are probably just myths. Even sorting out the terminology will help you as you begin to seek answers.

The information in **Living with a Functioning Alcoholic** could be useful to anyone dealing with a problem drinker. You could be a man with an alcohol-abusing wife. You could have a parent showing signs of alcohol abuse. You could be the parent of an adult child who is demonstrating problem drinking. Or you could simply have a friend who you think drinks too much.

Your Starting Point

But if you are a woman in a relationship with someone who you think at the very least is misusing alcohol, **Living with a Functioning Alcoholic - A Woman's Survival Guide** is your essential starting point.

As a woman you may still be wondering why Dr. Neill Neill, a man, would have written a book for women. I have written it because I see a need, and I believe I bring some unique qualifications and perspectives to the subject. You will better understand where I am coming from after you have read a couple more chapters.

Living with alcoholism in the family can be a very discouraging affair. **Chapter 2** is aimed at lifting you out of that discouragement. Your situation is what it is, but there is hope for the future.

Chapter 3 is about my past personal relationship with alcohol. I wanted you to know that *Living with a Functioning Alcoholic* arises from a great deal of personal and professional experience with alcoholism. Some of it was quite painful at the time; most of it has been hopeful.

Part Two deals with the basic facts and the myths about alcoholism and problem drinking. Signs and symptoms are discussed. Important distinctions are made. Part Two discusses disease, genetics, addiction, addictive personality, causes, dual diagnosis, functional alcoholism and more. And with the foundation of understanding you gain in Part Two, you will be able to sort through the misinformation and poor advice so free ly given.

Part Three deals with the repercussions of your partner's alcohol abuse for you and others. Topics include codependency, work, financial implications, the effects on your children and the general chaos of the alcoholic family. One chapter is devoted to dealing with parents and in-laws who abuse alcohol. Easy reading on tough topics! As you read, I invite you to reflect on your own circumstances and role in the confusion of alcoholism.

Part Four moves on, not only to living with your alcohol-abusing partner, but also to helping him. Helping a functioning alcoholic is a complex process, and Part Four will help you avoid the land mines. Two chapters are devoted to your own self-care, which is critical to your being able to help your partner.

Part Five, the final section, is devoted to getting outside help for your partner when he has acknowledged he may have a drinking problem and has expressed an interest in making a change.

Topics include the issue of "cure," detoxification services, *Alcoholics Anonymous*, a number of alternatives to AA, alcohol and drug treatment centers, and individualized therapeutic programs. Part Five ends with seven major recommendations to guide you and your partner in selecting treatment. **Chapter 2** is about hope.

Your greatest legacy to your family is your_____ of how you lived your life.

Reflection: Am I limiting my life and sense of well-being by my partner's alcohol abuse? How?

Chapter 2
A Book About Hope

I wrote *Living with a Functioning Alcoholic* to help women who are living with alcohol abuse in their families. I see such women in my psychological counseling practice, of course. They usually leave with renewed hope and a menu of practical avenues for sorting out their problems.

But for each woman I see in my practice there are dozens more who are unable to afford therapy, but are suffering the same problems. Most will never get to see a professional. They go on suffering great distress, often until their relationship finally disintegrates.

Then there is the problem of distance. Every week somebody telephones or emails me with a problem, but lives too far away to be able to come to my office.

I wrote *Living with a Functioning Alcoholic* to help the many women living in the chaos of alcoholic families, for whom going to a psychologist cannot be their first step. *Living with a Functioning Alcoholic* can help them get some clarity and perspective on what is going on in their lives.

As I said in the previous chapter, there is a great deal of misinformation in the field of alcoholism and its treatment. People have strong opinions. People carry beliefs about alcohol that haven't been true for 50 years. Perhaps they were never true.

The facts about alcohol use and misuse are poorly understood; for example, do you understand the difference between alcohol abuse and alcoholism? What is the difference between an alcoholic and a functioning alcoholic? A good understanding does make a difference!

The underlying message you need to get is this: There is hope! There is always hope!

Things may not be as bad as you think. Things are not as hopeless as you think. There are steps you can take. You don't have to be a victim. Nor is your partner a victim, no matter what conventional wisdom seems to suggest.

You are reading **Living with a Functioning Alcoholic - A Woman's Survival Guide** because your partner is abusing alcohol. My hope for you is that you will gain enough awareness and understanding to take the necessary steps towards a better life for yourself and your partner.

Spiritual Issues

You are dealing with big life issues, not just a practical problem. You are searching for meaning and purpose. You are dealing with connection and alienation. As such you are dealing with spiritual issues.

You are, of course, dealing with behavioral and psychological issues too. You may be dealing with issues of physical health as well. You are coping with the practical problems of life because you have to survive.

But whether or not you have any religious beliefs or practices, it is always good to remember that healing and growth have a spiritual side.

You are living with a problem drinker. His drinking may be in part his way of coping with big spiritual issues of life he is facing. He does not have to be conscious of this for it to be true.

If you have religious faith, avail yourself of pastoral counseling or whatever other support your religious group may provide. A great deal of support and uplifting of spirits may be available to you just for the asking. Meditate and pray if you can.

I would invite you to tap into all of the help you can get from whatever source. But first educate yourself with **Living with a Functioning Alcoholic** so you won't be led down so many blind alleys.

There is always_____.

Reflection: What big-picture life issues have I been neglecting?

Chapter 3
Neill's Personal Story of Entanglement with Alcohol

I too have been touched by alcohol. But before you can appreciate the story of my bout with alcoholism, you need to know a bit about my early background.

Shaky Beginnings

I was the oldest of four boys and we were quite poor.

At age four I was abducted, sexually abused, tortured and left for dead. At age seven I was again abducted and sexually abused.

At the time of the latter incident, my father was away working at a remote northern weather station in the Canadian Arctic. He had been sent there on threat of losing his job. He had to stay for two years, and then was killed in a plane crash on his way home. I was eight.

My mother never remarried, and she supported us boys by taking in sewing. Then, when I was 16, she was killed in a car crash by a drinking driver.

There wasn't any alcohol in our home as I grew up. Mother did not drink. Nor did any of my grandparents. Most of my mother's brothers didn't drink.

I married a non-drinker at 20. We were both way too young and mixed-up to get married, and it was a difficult marriage. We had two beautiful children, one of whom died of liver disease and cancer in 2006.

Divorce was not an option within our belief systems. No one in either of our extended families had ever divorced. With great pain we split up after ten years and the entrance of a new man.

Towards the end of that marriage I began to drink. After our marriage broke down, I was separated from my kids. My drinking kept increasing.

Enter Alcohol Abuse

Sometime later I remarried and adopted four more children. I held a good job as a university teacher.

By my mid-thirties, I was consuming a lot of alcohol every day. I might start with a drink or two with my lunch. Then after work at home I would have a cocktail or two before dinner and one or two bottles of wine with my wife at dinner. I would then keep the brandy or scotch or rum flowing throughout the evening.

By the time I crashed into bed I would have consumed the equivalent of 18 to 20 ounces of pure alcohol. Clearly, I was abusing alcohol, although I was not really aware I had a problem.

Other than the excessive consumption, I wasn't stupid with my drinking. My family was not deprived of anything materially. Since I would never drink and drive, my drinking didn't get me into trouble with the law. I never got hangovers and I seldom got drunk.

Unfortunately, the children were certainly deprived of my participation. Once I had begun to drink, I would not drive.

And if my children needed a lift somewhere, they were out of luck. This happened a lot.

Enter Health Problems

Four years into our marriage my wife had become very worried about my health. I was ill with increasing frequency.

My doctor thought I had a duodenal ulcer, and then that I was having a gallbladder attack. He also thought I had a hernia. Then he sent me off to have my heart tested.

Finally, after several hospitalizations I went to the Mayo Clinic in Minnesota to find out where all these symptoms were coming from. It turned out that I had probably become allergic to alcohol.

From Twenty Ounces to Zero

At that point in my life I was pretty naïve about the practical aspects of alcoholism and addiction. Even though the Addiction Research Foundation of Ontario supported me financially during my graduate studies, and even though I was teaching psychology at university level, my practical knowledge was limited.

When the Mayo Clinic specialists told me what was happening, I just quit drinking. Consumption went from twenty ounces of liquor a day to zero without a hiccup. I didn't know it was supposed to be difficult to quit.

Within a month I felt better than I had in years. That was over thirty years ago.

Understanding Comes Later

A few years later, while I was studying in an MBA program at University of Ottawa, I did some research on government attempts to promote safety around alcohol. This got me into the government statistics on alcohol consumption and abuse.

When I did some retrospective analysis of what I had been drinking, I was horrified to find I had been drinking at the level of the skid-row alcoholic. My alcohol problem had been much more serious than I had ever realized.

Sometime later my alcohol education got another jolt. Of my nine children (biological, adopted and stepchildren) several got into serious addiction problems as adults.

My stepson Colin, who had been in my life since he was 11, died of heart failure in early 2008. His heart failure was a complication of long-term alcohol and drug addiction. He was 40.

If you don't already know this, believe me when I say that being a parent of an alcoholic/addict provides a whole new perspective on alcoholism.

Private Practice

In the early 90's my private practice was focused on trauma counseling. I later returned to private practice after serving for a few years as psychologist for an aboriginal health and addiction treatment center. Along with my private practice I am Consulting Psychologist for the Sunshine Coast Health Centre, a private alcohol and drug rehab facility for men.

Many troubled people come to me with drug- and alcohol-related problems. And many more spouses of functioning alcoholics come for help in sorting out their lives.

Nothing is as it seems. The whole field is fraught with myths, half-truths and beliefs, many of which are vehemently defended but are misguided and serve little useful purpose. Some of the misinformation about alcoholism actually makes the problem worse.

The culture of alcoholism and recovery is fertile ground for mistakes, half-truths, slogans and strongly held beliefs with little basis in fact.

Part Two deals with the basics of alcoholism and brings some of the myths to the forefront. My goal is to help you get some clarity as to what is fact and what is myth or speculation. Where there is genuine controversy, I attempt to provide both sides so that you can be better informed as you draw your own conclusions.

Remember, clarity is the key to regaining your personal power.

Reflection: Has anyone in your circle of family and friends had a loved one die of causes related to alcohol abuse? Is anyone you know at risk now?

Part Two
What You Need to Know About Alcoholism and Alcohol Abuse

Chapter 4
Does Your Partner Have an Alcohol Problem?

Signs and Symptoms of Alcohol Abuse

In this section, I cover the most common problems and characteristics that are associated with problem drinking. For the purposes of this chapter I do not make specific distinctions among the terms problem drinking, alcohol abuse, alcoholism, functional alcoholism and alcohol dependence. In later chapters, I will make some practical distinctions.

- **Your partner admits he could have a drinking problem.**

An important sign of problem drinking is the drinker occasionally admitting he has a problem with alcohol. If it is creeping into his consciousness enough for him to raise the question, his drinking probably is a problem.

But it does not always mean there is a problem. I have worked with people so traumatized by parental alcohol abuse early in their lives that they begin to think they have an alcohol problem when they are consuming only a glass of wine every other day.

So even when he says "I may have a drinking problem," it is a good idea to look at the situation more carefully. In the field of alcohol abuse, people are often quick to label. Don't do it.

31

- **You think your partner could be an alcoholic.**

If you think he could be an alcoholic, you might be right. But you could be wrong for the same reason as he could be wrong, as mentioned above. So go deeper.

- **He drinks every day.**

If your partner drinks every day, even moderately, he could be developing alcohol dependence. In some European countries where wine is served at almost every meal, there is a higher-than-average frequency of cirrhosis of the liver. So just because a person doesn't get drunk does not mean there is no problem. If he drinks every day, a health problem and an addiction could be developing, as it was in my case.

The principle to understand is that if he is becoming dependent on alcohol or if alcohol is affecting his health, then he does have a drinking problem.

- **He drinks only periodically, but he gets drunk when he does drink.**

He consumes alcohol only on weekends, for example, but to excess most times. That is the pattern of the "weekend drunk," the binge drinker. So even when he is not drinking every day, he may still have a very serious drinking problem.

- **Your partner sometimes drives his car or operates machinery while under the influence of alcohol.**

If he drinks, even occasionally, before driving a vehicle or operating machinery, he has a drinking problem. In this context, I am not talking about whether or not he is over the legal limit.

The case of the airplane pilot illustrates this point. Pilots have a saying, which comes from their flight training: "**twelve hours from bottle to throttle**." Alcohol affects eyesight, judgment, ability to adapt to pressure changes and ability to focus. The effects are enough that any amount of alcohol in his system puts the pilot, his airplane and his passengers at risk.

The fact is that many people drink a little, and then drive. That is our cultural history. But our culture is clearly moving in the direction of zero tolerance. It is already there for new drivers in some jurisdictions.

I predict that we will see zero tolerance for alcohol while driving in the foreseeable future, and I don't think it's just wishful thinking.

- **His drinking has led to legal problems.**

Impaired driving (DUI) charges mean he has a drinking problem. That's obvious. But assault charges or domestic violence charges could also be indicators of a serious drinking problem.

- **Your partner has put obtaining alcohol ahead of the purchase of family necessities.**

Is there a shortage of money in the household, due in part to alcohol being given a higher priority than food or clothing or children's activities? If yes, you are witnessing problem drinking.

- **His drinking has contributed to a chaotic, dysfunctional family environment.**

You feel like you're walking on eggshells when you're dealing with him. There is arguing and blaming going on in the household. Your partner expresses a lot of anger and defensiveness, especially when drinking. There may be threats and raging. This volatility is often followed by apologies the next day.

All these are indications of two things. First, there is a clear presence of problem drinking. Secondly, there is a clear presence of codependence. Your family has entered the alcoholic dance. I discuss the alcoholic dance in more detail in Chapter 16.

- **Your partner exhibits a deep unhappiness and drinks to feel better.**

This symptom of alcohol abuse may be viewed as spiritual and/or psychological. Many, if not most, problem drinkers exhibit a deep unhappiness, often labeled "depression." Depression is a condition of separation. The individual feels separated from other people and separated from God. He experiences it as a profound disconnection, a disenfranchisement from life.

- **He says he needs a drink to build up his self-confidence.**

Self-esteem often takes a beating when people begin to drink too much. It is usually difficult or impossible to tell whether the drinking or the low self-esteem came first. My guess is the more often than not low self esteem leads to drinking, which in turn leads to the further lowering of self esteem.

Conclusion

All these characteristics tend to make for chaotic living. The chaotic household—and I am not talking about lack of tidiness—is one of the earmarks of an alcoholic family. When the children grow up, their universal chorus is, "I grew up in a dysfunctional family."

So far I have deliberately made no attempt to distinguish between "alcohol abuse" and "alcoholism." People use these terms interchangeably in casual conversation. However, there are important, practical distinctions to make, and you will become clear about them as you read the next few chapters.

Reflection: Of the 10 signs and symptoms, how may apply to your situation?

Further Reflection: What are you feeling when he disappears into alcohol, when he's there, but not present?

Chapter 5
Problem Drinking
and Alcohol Abuse:
Is There a Difference?

The phrases "problem drinking" and "alcohol abuse" can refer to any kind of drinking that has negative effects on the drinker or on those around him. *Living with a Functioning Alcoholic* uses the two terms interchangeably. If I say problem drinking, read alcohol abuse, and vice versa.

A Definition of Problem Drinking

If a person's drinking leads to impairment or to health, social, legal, employment, family, or financial problems, it is considered to be problem drinking. The form of the drinking does not matter; that is, it could be any of moderate social drinking, heavy regular drinking, binging or addictive drinking. Whether a person's alcohol use can be considered alcohol abuse (problem drinking) depends entirely on the effects of the drinking. These effects may be poor judgment, memory lapses, interference with job or education, deteriorating social skills, neglect of family and chaotic family life.

Let's look at the definition to see how it may play out in real life.

Given my allergic reaction to alcohol, a glass of wine once a week would for me be problem drinking or alcohol abuse, because it would have a bad effect on my health. And it would be damned uncomfortable! A day and a half after a glass of wine I would have the kind of pain I imagine I'd have after a hard kick in the groin. (Did I mention I don't drink anymore?)

For someone else, drinking a daily glass of wine with dinner, or regularly having a beer on coming home from work might not be a problem at all.

Examples of Alcohol Abuse

- If a man is periodically absent from work because of hangovers, he is abusing alcohol.

- If a student's memory is affected by going out for a few drinks on Friday night, the student has an alcohol-abuse problem. (A good memory is critical to being a successful student.)

- If there is money to buy alcohol, but not enough to buy groceries, there is alcohol abuse.

- If drinking leads to domestic violence, it's alcohol abuse.

- If drinking leads to conflict with the law, it's alcohol abuse.

I hope you are getting the picture. Whether or not your partner's drinking is to be considered alcohol abuse is determined by looking at the effects of his drinking—financial, mental, legal, social, family and health.

You determine whether drink has become alcohol abuse by its _____.

Reflection: Using the definition in this chapter, is your partner abusing alcohol? Has it gotten worse over time?

Chapter 6
How Can Alcohol Use Become Voluntary Dissociation?

Consider what it means to feel whole, to have your mind, body and spirit function as a unit. This ideal state of wholeness indicates wellness in the full sense of the word.

Wholeness is the main goal of many therapies, including the energy psychology therapy I practice. It is also the goal of most spiritual pursuits. Wholeness encourages better self-care, perspective, wisdom, happiness and fulfillment.

The Opposite of Wholeness

Dissociation, on the other hand, is a disruption in wholeness. In psychology it is thought of as a disruption in the functions of consciousness, memory or identity. Increasingly we are expanding the meaning to include disruptions not just in the psyche but in the physical body and the spirit as well.

The word "dissociation" comes from "dis," meaning "the opposite of," and "association."

If wholeness is the bringing together of everything, dissociation is the disruption of that integration.

Dissociation shows up in our everyday language and experience. Have you ever found yourself doing something and then later saying, "I wasn't myself," "I don't know what got into me," or "That was out of character for me?" Of course you have. We all dissociate sometimes.

Dissociation can be in the spiritual realm too, showing up as a feeling of profound disconnection and meaninglessness. It is often labeled depression. The refrain is, "I have no meaningful future." This is also the refrain of the alcoholic.

In Western cultures often we are encouraged to dissociate from our bodies in order to keep up a frenetic pace. Not wanting to face our distress, we may store it as high blood pressure, heart disease, breathing problems, muscle tension, headaches, sexual dysfunction, irritable bowel syndrome, digestive problems and perhaps even cancer.

Have you ever maintained your dissociation by saying "It's just my body; it's not me?"

I have been guilty of such denial—I held onto an old resentment and maintained it as a chronic stomach ailment for over half a century. Seven years ago when I became conscious of what I was doing, it took less than an hour of energy psychology to eliminate my stomach problem permanently.

Our culture strongly encourages us to take pills, inhale substances and drink alcohol to help us dissociate from the physical pains, heartaches and anxieties of life. If we can just separate ourselves from these interferences, we think life will be better.

Your partner is exposed to all these influences just like everyone else is. Unfortunately, for whatever reasons, his attempts to feel better have led to alcohol abuse and perhaps alcohol addiction.

The Bottom Line

Think of his alcohol use as voluntary dissociation. Drinking allows him to escape from feelings of pain or isolation or inadequacy by dissociating from himself. But while he is dissociated from his feelings through alcohol, he is less than a whole person.

Voluntary dissociation, in whatever form, is alien to wholeness of spirit, body and psyche.

My belief is that wholeness beats dissociation every time. Let yourself be conscious of the psychological, physical or spiritual pain. It is telling you that you have some personal work to do, and where to start.

By the same token, your partner will start to work on himself when he allows himself to become more conscious of his pain and reduces his drinking. Without consciousness, change is unlikely.

Reflection: Be curious about the pull between voluntary dissociation and and wholeness in your own life.

Chapter 7
Alcoholism Defined

T he word "alcoholism" in general usage has at least two meanings.

The Broad Meaning of Alcoholism

Alcoholism is a term used to describe the broad field of problem drinking, alcohol abuse, alcohol dependence, alcohol addiction, functional alcoholism and all of the accompanying behaviors and symptoms.

Living with a Functioning Alcoholic broadly refers to alcoholism in this general sense. It covers many aspects of the field of alcoholism, including treatment.

The Narrow Meaning of "Alcoholism"

The second meaning of alcoholism is much more specific. *Alcoholism* in the narrower sense means alcohol dependence[1]. The definition comes from the **DSM-IV**, the North American bible for the diagnosis of mental disorders.

Up to this point the broad view of alcoholism has worked in the discussion. But from this point on when I refer to someone as *an alcoholic*, I am using the term to mean alcohol

[1] The *Diagnostic and Statistical Manual of Mental Disorders (DSM-IV)* of the American Psychiatric Association. p. 195.

dependent. Whether he is a skid-row alcoholic or a high-functioning alcoholic is irrelevant to the definition.

The **DSM-IV** discussion of alcohol-related disorders does not even use the term "alcoholism" or "alcoholic." Rather, they refer to a mental disorder called **"alcohol dependence."** Alcohol dependence may be with or without physical dependence.

The Four Features of Alcohol Dependence

Most descriptions of alcohol dependence feature four major criteria. If any of these are present, the **DSM-IV** considers it to be "alcohol dependence."

1. **Craving**. The alcohol-dependent person craves alcohol. He has a psychological compulsion to drink alcohol. He seems driven to acquire and consume alcohol.

2. **Loss of Control**. Alcohol dependence is usually characterized by a loss of control. If offered a drink, he cannot refuse. Once the person starts to drink, he can't stop. No matter what his intentions were to start with, he seems to lack the ability to limit his drinking once he starts.

For some alcoholics this means continuing to drink until there is nothing more to drink. For others it means drinking until unconscious. The amount of alcohol required to reach intoxication varies widely from person to person.

3.   **Physical Dependence.** The third characteristic of alcoholism is physical dependence on alcohol. It is not always present in alcoholism, but it usually is. If the physically-dependent alcoholic is deprived of alcohol, he may have a variety of symptoms such as nausea, shakiness, sweating or even hallucinations, during the period of **withdrawal**.

Such physical symptoms are more likely to occur after a period of heavy drinking. Typically, withdrawal also involves psychological symptoms such as anxiety and fear.

Note: Some psychological symptoms may persist long after the acute withdrawal phase has passed. The post-acute withdrawal phase, the 'dry drunk' phase, is discussed further in Chapter 33.

4.   **Tolerance**. The fourth symptom associated with alcohol dependence is tolerance. Most alcoholics have developed a high tolerance for alcohol. This could mean one of several things.

- Over time the alcoholic has needed to consume greater and greater quantities of alcohol to get the desired effects.

- Alternatively, he consumes very large amounts of alcohol with little apparent effect.

- As the alcoholism progresses, it takes less and less alcohol consumption to produce signs of intoxication.

Is He an Alcoholic?

I had a work friend once whom I'll call Dan. Dan would drink five double martinis for lunch and go back to one-on-one work with clients in the afternoon. He would drink at least that much at the club after work before his wife would come to pick him up for dinner. Yet I never saw him drunk.

It was unclear whether he ever lost control. And how much he craved alcohol was unknown because he was never deprived of it. He was affluent enough that acquiring alcohol was apparently not a financial strain.

Dan saw himself as an alcoholic who had a very high level of physical dependence and a very high tolerance. More on Dan later.

In my own case I would have twelve to fourteen drinks of hard stuff a day, sometimes more, sometimes a bit less. That is certainly evidence of high tolerance. By the **DSM-IV** definition the presence of high tolerance would have classified me as alcohol dependent.

I'm not sure how strongly I craved alcohol, because I always had it. I don't think there was a loss of control, because I could stop whenever I wanted to, and I did stop whenever there was a reason for doing so.

Furthermore, I may not have been physically dependent. I experienced no withdrawal symptoms when I switched instantly from twenty ounces of alcohol a day to none at all. And I never got hangovers after drinking heavily. However, there is no question I was an alcoholic, slowly killing myself.

Is my partner an alcoholic? If that is your question, don't be too quick to brand him "an alcoholic." Labeling seldom accomplishes anything positive. On the other hand, do be up-front in speaking to him about the effects of his drinking.

Remember, all alcoholics are problem drinkers. Only some problem drinkers have become alcoholics.

The next chapter deals with the subject of the functioning alcoholic.

The four major criteria for alcohol dependence are craving, loss of control, physical dependence and_____. Any one of these indicates alcohol dependence.

Reflection: How well does your partner fit the medical definition of "alcohol dependent?" Did you know that alcohol dependence is classified as a Mental Disorder?

Chapter 8
The Functioning Alcoholic

The title of the book is *Living with a Functioning Alcoholic - A Woman's Survival Guide,* so we need to look at the meaning of "functioning." Is there any real difference between an alcoholic and a functioning alcoholic?

The so-called functioning alcoholic may not fit the stereotype of the skid-row drunk, but he is an alcoholic nonetheless.

Among all the people drinking at a family picnic, a work party or at a happy-hour gathering of friends, a few will be full-blown alcoholics. They may drink a bit more than others, but generally they blend in with everyone else. After all, they hold jobs, serve on volunteer committees, have families and have friends. These are the so-called "functioning alcoholics."

So what's wrong with his being an alcoholic if he can function normally? He will certainly ask the question with an expectation of the obvious answer, 'nothing.'

The first thing to realize is that his job or profession isn't his only function. Two famous entertainers come to mind, a very popular late-night TV host and a famous singer-entertainer: both were functioning alcoholics, but both were known to be wife beaters. Since when is beating your wife considered to be functioning?

We are all aware of other public examples, like the successful political leader charged with impaired driving, or the wealthy professional who abandons his family, claiming poverty.

Multiply the public examples of alcoholic dysfunction in some aspect of life by a thousand, and you get a picture of the neglect, abuse, lies and cover-up that are out there among the population of "functioning" alcoholics.

The second thing to understand about the functioning alcoholic is that he may be functioning far below potential, even at work, the area where he claims to be functioning.

During my own alcoholic period, I did my job adequately and I was a kind loving father. But I will never know whether I might have started writing earlier in my career, were it not for the drink. What I do know is I never went to any of my kid's games or took them camping during that period, and I didn't even become aware of the neglect until it was too late. It was as if my life was on hold for a few years.

I knew a 21-year-old woman who had the dream of becoming a doctor and the energy and brains to do it. Like many students, she had to take a work break from her studies. While she worked in a bar to get the money together, drinking crept into her daily routine. Now over 50 and four marriages later she's still working in a bar, her dream of being a doctor, a distant memory.

The third failure of the functioning alcoholic has to do with how long the functioning alcoholic lasts, that is, how long he lives. Alcohol was affecting my health. If I hadn't stopped I would have been dead years ago. And what I have brought to others in the past thirty years would simply never have existed.

Remeber Dan? He was a brilliant psychiatrist at a university student counselling center. He would go back to a productive afternoon after his five-double-martini lunch. But he left his wife and children and potentially thousands more young clients by dying of liver cancer far too young.

The notion of a functioning alcoholic, it seems to me, is an oxymoron. To function is to function in life, not just in one part of life. Functioning means fulfilling your potential and pursuing your dreams as best you can. And functioning is a long-term matter, not just a temporary condition.

If your car would run, but wouldn't go up hill, was unsafe to drive on the roads and might last another month at most, would you think of it as a "functioning automobile?" I doubt it. Your *For Sale* ad would read, *"Runs. As is. To be towed away."*

When I apply the same reasoning to the alcoholic, I have to conclude that I have never met a true functioning alcoholic. And I certainly wasn't one.

And yet I use the term in the title of this book. I hear people at AA meetings say, "I was a functioning alcoholic." My women clients often lead off with "My husband is a functioning alcoholic." The notion of the functioning alcoholic is so much a part of the culture of alcoholism that I have to use it to communicate.

But make no mistake: a man who is addicted to and dependent on alcohol is an alcoholic, whether or not he can keep a job or be good to his family. I hold "functioning" to a higher standard than just "getting by."

In the next chapter I discuss the "stages of alcoholism." You may be surprised.

Reflection: How do you use the word "functioning?" Do you use it to mean functioning in all three aspects, or just getting by?

Further Reflection: Could putting the word "functioning" in front of "alcoholic" be just an easy way of dealing with a serious (mental) health problem?

Chapter 9
Stages of Alcoholism:
Reality or Myth?

The notion of there being *stages of alcoholism* is misleading. Referring to the narrow definition of alcoholism from the *Chapter 7*, there can be only one stage, that of alcohol dependence. My sense is that the concept of stages of alcoholism may be just a convenient myth.

Talking about the stages of alcoholism is a bit like saying that infancy, childhood, adolescence and adulthood are *stages of adulthood*. It seems silly when put this way.

The notion of stages comes from the fact that there are different levels of alcohol use and abuse. The different levels may precede alcohol dependence. For most people the early "stages" never lead anywhere, making it inappropriate to even call them stages.

So the early "stages of alcoholism" are really not stages of alcoholism, but patterns of drinking that in a minority of cases will evolve into addiction to alcohol.

Nevertheless, you should be familiar with what people are talking about when they refer to stages of alcoholism.

1. **Stage One**. With the above disclaimers, the first of these so-called stages is simply the use of alcohol.

    People drink alcohol, and they don't have any particular negative consequences. It's having a beer after work, or having a glass of wine with dinner, or participating in a toast at a wedding.

2. **Stage Two**. The popular notion is that the drinker is at the second stage of alcoholism when he begins to experience negative consequences from using alcohol.

    The negative consequences could be severe or minor, but the severity is not the point. The point is that a *pattern* of negative consequences of drinking is developing.

I knew a young man who was a very light drinker. After a big argument with his wife, he gulped down a few drinks and went for a drive. He was stopped and charged with impaired driving. The consequences of his one-time misuse of alcohol were quite severe. In his case I would not consider him to be at Stage Two, because there is no pattern of negative consequences. It happened only once.

3. **Stage Three**. The third so-called stage is continued abuse of alcohol. This involves continued use of alcohol in spite of the negative consequences. If the young man I just spoke of were to become intoxicated and drive again when upset, I would consider his behavior to be alcohol abuse.

I was abusing alcohol. But once I discovered that I had become allergic to alcohol, I stopped drinking. If I had continued to drink in spite of what I knew, it would have represented a big increase in my level of alcohol abuse.

Everything I have said so far about the stages of alcoholism or the stages of drinking leading up to alcoholism falls short of alcoholism.

4.   **Stage Four**. The fourth stage is alcohol dependence or addiction. It's the compulsive seeking and use of alcohol, regardless of the negative consequences it has.

I saw in the newspaper the other day that police had stopped a driver for not wearing a seatbelt. They then found he was drunk and charged him with driving under the influence of alcohol. They also discovered that his license was already under suspension for driving under the influence of alcohol. I would speculate that this man is dependent on alcohol and drinks compulsively.

The (stage four) alcoholic is the man who continues to drink, even though he knows that when he drinks he gets belligerent, gets in fights, gets arrested for disorderly conduct or spousal assault, suffers deteriorating health, or at the very least, makes poor judgments.

I knew a small-town doctor once who drank so compulsively that he was often drunk while providing medical services. A former patient of his told me he was so drunk that two hospital staff members had to hold him up while he delivered her last two babies.

The One Stage of Alcoholism

It should be clear by now that the notion of stages of alcoholism is at the very least a misnomer. Only the fourth so-called stage is actually alcohol dependence. The earlier drinking patterns precede alcoholism, but only in a minority of cases do they actually lead to alcohol dependence.

The use and then abuse of alcohol seldom lead to alcoholism. A pattern of continued alcohol abuse presents more of a risk. If alcohol abuse is continued for a prolonged period of time, there is a substantial possibility that the abuse will develop into full-blown alcohol **dependence**, including physical dependence.

I suspect the majority of people who abuse alcohol never actually become physically dependent alcoholics. More often than not they begin to recognize the problem and deal with it before they become physically addicted.

My last comment, of course, is speculative. It is not a simple matter to decide with any assurance that a particular alcohol abuser is physically alcohol dependent. If he continues doing what he is doing, there is no easy way to tell. It is after he stops drinking and begins to deal with the effects of stopping that we can make a more reliable assessment. And I think many alcoholics understand this, at least at an unconscious level.

I suspect there are quite a few alcoholics out there who may privately speculate they have a serious alcohol problem and are physically dependent. But as long as they don't quit drinking and as long as they don't get into too much trouble, that is, as long as they are "functioning," they won't have to quit drinking and find out whether or not they are physically addicted.

Alcoholism is a progressive disorder, but more about this later.

Reflection: What, if anything, would lead you to suspect your partner doesn't attempt to quit because he might be physically addicted and is afraid of failure?

Chapter 10
Alcoholism As a Disease: Reality or Myth?

The debate over whether alcoholism is a disease has raged for over two hundred years. An American physician, Benjamin Rush, M.D., is credited with first calling alcoholism a disease in 1784.

AA and the Disease Concept of Alcoholism

AA is widely believed to have popularized the notion of alcoholism as a disease. This was not the intent of its cofounder Bill Wilson. When he was asked about his position on the disease concept, he said in 1960,

> *We have never called alcoholism a disease because, technically speaking, it is not a disease entity. For example, there is no such thing as heart disease. Instead there are many separate heart ailments, or combinations of them. It is something like that with alcoholism. Therefore, we did not wish to get in wrong with the medical profession by*
>
> *pronouncing alcoholism a disease entity. Therefore, we always call it an illness, or a malady—a far safer term for us to use.*[2]

---

[2] Wilson, Bill. Cited by White, W. L. The Rebirth of the Disease Concept of Alcoholism in the 20th Century. *Counselor Magazine*, 2000, p. 63

The other cofounder of AA, Dr. Bob Smith, said we "have to use disease. [It is the] only way to get across hopelessness."

To put it another way, Dr. Smith was saying that the use of the medical metaphor within AA was really a device to convince alcoholics that they could never drink again.

Apparently, neither Bill Wilson nor Dr. Bob Smith really believed that alcoholism was a disease like any other disease. Nevertheless the disease concept of alcoholism is alive and well within the AA movement. That was not AA's intent. Its goal was to help alcoholics.

The Debate Continues, but Is There Light?

The strongest modern advocate of alcoholism as a disease was Elvin Jellinek, who published the book *The Disease Concept of Alcoholism* in 1960.

It is useful to recall that the DSM-IV describes a mental disorder called "alcohol dependence," and another called "alcohol abuse."

Both are mental disorders. In fact, according to the DSM-IV they are among the most common adult mental disorders in society.

The problem with calling alcoholism a disease is that it carries the implication that alcoholism is a single medical disorder. Scientific research has never borne this out.

The phrase "disease of alcoholism" is certainly a part of popular culture, but alcoholism is not a disease entity in any medical sense.

Does It Matter?

In order to make any sense out of this whole debate, we have to look beyond the labels. I suggest that what is important for our present purposes is to understand how to help people with drinking problems.

Dr. Smith used the disease metaphor to convince alcoholic derelicts that they had to stop drinking completely or they would die.

Recent research done in Australia has shed some light on the issue:

> *Results indicated that those subjects who held the disease concept regarding their drug use were in general more psychologically depressed and their levels of psychological functioning were less adaptive and less positive that individuals who held a non-disease orientation. These results may indicate that more adaptive psychological functioning can be achieved by teaching clients a learned habit orientation rather than a disease concept.*[3]

Their findings indicate that those who believed they were the victim of the disease of alcoholism did not function as well in life as those who believed they had learned some bad habits (alcohol abuse) and therefore they could learn better habits. They had a sense of being in control.

Social psychologist Stanton Peele wrote a book called **Diseasing of America**. Dr. Peele views alcoholism as a personal conduct problem rather than a disease. He presents some very potent arguments against the disease concept. More importantly, he presents many instances of people being harmed in the name of treatment for a disease.

---

[3] Granger, J. and Farina, M. Attributions regarding the causes of alcoholism and psychological functioning. Paper presented at 1998 Conference: *Addictions: Challenges and Changes.*

Dr. Peele's view of alcoholism is more prevalent among the medical profession than it is within the general public. A recent Gallup poll suggested that almost ninety percent of Americans accept alcoholism as a disease. In contrast, in a survey of physicians it was found that eighty percent of the doctors who responded perceived alcoholism simply as bad behavior.

A Practical Compromise

I don't regard people with drinking problems as either diseased or bad. We need a more practical way to look at alcohol abuse.

Avoid the mistake of allowing the problem drinker to think he is the victim of a disease, and therefore not responsible. Avoid also the mistake of making problem drinking totally a moral issue. The latter would be a way of making somebody bad. Simply labeling someone as bad or diseased doesn't help him or anyone else.

If an alcoholic in recovery says "I can never drink because my alcoholism is a disease I'll have for life," I encourage him in his sobriety. His belief in alcoholism as a disease is supporting his resolve to abstain and to make sobriety a part of his lifestyle. On a very practical level, the behavior flowing from his belief could be saving his life.

If a practicing alcoholic, on the other hand, says "I can't help myself because I have the disease of alcoholism and it's incurable," I challenge his belief. He is using the disease notion to justify his continuing alcohol abuse. For such a person the disease notion is counterproductive to any practical steps to recovery.

Having said that, I question whether the disease metaphor is practical when attempting to help problem drinkers who are not yet alcohol dependent. It could end up harming as many as it might help.

The next chapter tackles the possible genetic roots of alcoholism. You will see how genetic explanations carry some of the same shortcomings as do disease explanations.

***

Reflection: Have people you know used the disease concept to justify their continued drinking? Have others used it to justify their not drinking? If "yes" to both, does it make sense to you?

Chapter 11
Is Alcoholism Genetic?

There is no question that problem drinking does run in families.

Many studies have tried to establish the presence of an actual genetic link. The research results suggest that there may be some genetic markers; that is, there may be some genetic predisposition to alcohol addiction.

However it is very clear that there are many behavioral, social and environmental factors which have a much larger effect on whether or not a person might eventually become dependent on alcohol.

Some studies show, for example, that antisocial personality disorder also runs in families, and these families exhibit a lot of alcohol abuse.

Clearly, we are a long way from understanding what causes what.

There will be more discussion of the causes of alcoholism in **Chapter 13**.

Trying to explain alcohol dependence through genetics carries the same risk as trying to explain it as a disease. There is a risk that the alcohol abuser will blame his genes for his drinking, conclude that he is a victim of his genetics, and therefore take no responsibility for his continuing to drink.

You have heard it before: "What would you expect? I get my alcoholism honestly—both my parents were alcoholics."

Essential to any good treatment program is the will of the drinker to help himself and to get whatever outside help is needed. Often one of the first steps in his deciding to seek help is accepting the fact that he is not controlled by his genetics. He does have a choice!

He can't beat his alcohol problem
until he really wants to.

The practical question to ask is whether acknowledging the genetic factor can help a problem drinker change.

If your partner is actively abusing alcohol, whether or not he is alcohol dependent, the genetics concept may do more harm than good. He could use it as just one more way to argue that he is a victim. As you will see in Chapter 16, you too could be using genetics to excuse his alcohol abuse.

If your partner is no longer abusing alcohol, the genetics factor is, of course, irrelevant.

Denial

A very strong characteristic of the problem drinker is his masterful use of denial. It doesn't matter whether he occasionally abuses alcohol or is severely alcohol dependent. Denial is the standard tool the drinker uses to avoid changing his behavior. First he denies vehemently that he has a problem. Then he admits he may have a problem, but denies the seriousness. Then when he acknowledges the seriousness, he denies there is any possibility of dealing with it.

There is increasing evidence that long-term alcohol abuse damages or at least alters the brain. Furthermore, the brain effects can last for at least several years after the drinking stops. Delusional thinking, that is, the distortion of reality, is one of the principal effects of the brain alteration. Denial, minimizing and hiding are expressions of delusional thinking. Delusional thinking is a symptom of alcoholism.

Arming the drinker with a disease concept or a genetic explanation makes it easier for him to continue in his denial of reality.

A Call to Calm

Before ending this section it is important to emphasize the following:

Only a small proportion of the people who use and occasionally over-use alcohol actually move on to regular alcohol abuse. Of those who do, only a small proportion will eventually become alcohol dependent. Most will do something about their problem drinking before they become alcohol dependent.

One common symptom of alcoholism is _____ thinking.

Reflection: Can you think of people you know who used to abuse alcohol, but now drink at a very moderate level or hardly at all? How and why did they change? Could your partner do this too?

Chapter 12
The Addictive Personality:
A Myth?

Addictive or Merely Compulsive?

It is true that some people have a tendency to handle things compulsively. And it certainly is true that someone addicted to alcohol acts compulsively in seeking and consuming alcohol. It is also true that a former compulsive drinker may well have shifted to some other form of compulsive pursuit. Witness the almost comical compulsive consumption of coffee at AA meetings and conventions.

I knew a compulsive drinker who stopped drinking; but once the dust settled, he pursued his career with a vengeance and became a compulsive worker. His friends called him a workaholic. Once he stopped drinking, he also began to eat compulsively and gained weight.

This is the kind of behavior that has led to the label *addictive personality.*

Many people of diverse personality types, lifestyles, cultures and ages have compulsive tendencies. Most of them, however, never become alcoholics, food-aholics, workaholics or any other "aholic." Nor do most people, whether alcoholics or not, ever develop obsessive-compulsive disorder. This disorder is at the extreme end of the continuum, affecting less than one percent of the adult population.

Given the wide prevalence of mild to moderate obsessions and compulsions in the general population, it is easy to see how the notion of an addictive personality could become popular.

It is more useful, however, simply to recognize the wide prevalence of compulsive tendencies in the general population, and therefore among alcoholics. Why drinkers might drink compulsively is discussed in the next chapter as we discuss cause.

A Practical Conclusion

The concept of the *addictive personality* is not very useful in explaining why people drink or why some become addicted to alcohol. And worse, it shares some of the same problems with the disease and genetic explanations of alcoholism. Namely, it sounds like something you are born with or could catch, and therefore, could be a victim of.

Once again we are dealing with a concept that could assist alcoholics in continuing to deny responsibility for their problem drinking.

Any concept that supports a drinker's denial of responsibility should be left out of the process of helping him come to terms with his alcohol abuse.

Reflection: Why is the notion of addictive personality so popular?

Chapter 13
What Causes Alcohol Abuse and Alcoholism?

People have been looking for *the cause* of alcoholism since problem drinking began. So what do we understand at this point?

At a very basic level we know this: drinking alcohol causes alcoholism. Stated differently, drinking is the cause of problem drinking.

If we spell it out a little further, we could say that drinking is the cause of problem drinking, and continued problem drinking is the cause of alcoholism.

Unfortunately, such an explanation is too simple to be of much use, and it is not very satisfying.

What we do know is that long-term alcohol abuse can lead to alcohol dependence, both psychological and physical. We understand a lot less about why a minority of drinkers will move from occasional misuse of alcohol to alcohol abuse, and then why a minority of these will continue the abuse until they become dependent on alcohol.

The Proper Question

So the proper question is not what causes alcoholism. The much more appropriate and useful question is the following:

What are the factors that might lead a person to move from simple use and occasional misuse of alcohol to long-term alcohol abuse?

The following discussion includes socio-cultural factors, family culture factors, psychological factors and spiritual factors.

Socio-cultural Factors

Modern life puts huge pressures on people to drink. Alcohol is widely available. It is relatively inexpensive. The industry advertises widely and intensely. It especially targets young people, who are at a stage of brain development that fosters strong conformity to social norms. The brain of a young person still has years to go in its development.

Alcohol establishments are widespread from the smallest communities to the largest cities. For many people the bar, pub or club is the meeting place for social activities. Alcohol is packaged and promoted as the accompaniment of all celebration.

Celebration

When I was the psychologist for a Native alcohol and drug addiciton treatment center, a group of clients would graduate from the treatment program every six weeks. Those six weeks were filled with intensive group coaching and therapy, AA meetings, good nutrition and individual counseling. All of these things were aimed at helping the client go back into his or her community and not relapse into drinking.

The highlight of each six-week program was the graduation celebration, a community potluck dinner. I remember one particularly excited and happy group on their last day. They were busy preparing the hall for the celebration dinner. They made a banner with all their names on it and got clip art from the internet to decorate the banner.

Without realizing what they had done they decorated their banner with drinking symbols—wine glasses and bottles—because these represented celebration.

Drinking is so much a part of our culture that even people who had been in a six-week intensive alcohol-treatment program were not conscious of using drinking symbols for celebration.

Family Culture Factors

It is clear that many problem drinkers grow up in families where at least one parent abused alcohol. This does not establish cause, however, because it is also clear that many more people who grow up in alcoholic families do not develop alcohol-abuse problems.

All of the children who grow up in the chaos of an alcoholic family, however, are greatly affected by it. It shows up in their attitudes and behavior, their ability to function in relationships and their ability to parent.

Some of the children of alcoholics will grow up to copy their parents in the way they handle problems. They will abuse alcohol too. Others will grow up determined not to copy their parents' dysfunctional patterns; they will quite intentionally live alcohol-free.

We don't understand the causal links well enough to predict who is going to have an alcohol problem and who is not. We do know that adult children's behavior patterns tend to be similar to the behavior patterns of their parents, at least during the young adulthood years.

If one or both parents escape into alcohol, the children are at greater risk of growing up to do the same. When the parents model escaping their problems rather than facing them, the children have less opportunity to learn more constructive and resourceful ways of handling problems.

A lot of alcoholic families are characterized by antisocial personality tendencies or borderline personality characteristics. Such families provide their children an environment for learning to use alcohol to deal with life's ups and downs. They increase the likelihood that their children will abuse alcohol as adults.

Psychological Factors

There is a lot of stress in our society and it causes physical problems like heart attacks, cancer and obesity. Treatment for stress is a multibillion-dollar per year enterprise.

A small amount of alcohol tends to reduce the unpleasantness of stress. It helps people relax. Socially, alcohol is an "ice-breaker." It is a pleasant way to unwind at the end of a day.

The stress response is hard-wired into all of us to save our lives in emergencies. Stress was never intended to be chronic. Our bodies are not designed to handle chronic stress. When stress becomes chronic and alcohol is always available as a relaxant, many people become habitual drinkers.

Reliance on alcohol for relief from various psychological stressors is a possible cause of problem drinking. The psychological underpinnings of alcohol use and abuse are treated more fully in the following chapter.

Spiritual Factors

Depression is a disorder with many different symptoms. A major symptom of depression is a feeling of separateness, a feeling of isolation, a feeling of profound disconnection. It's a lonely place. If you are living with an alcoholic, you have probably been there yourself. Depression is often thought of as a spiritual disease.

The opposite of separateness is a sense of connection with other people, with the universe, with God. This is a place of wholeness and wellness.

I believe that human beings have a built-in need to seek connection. When people experience separateness and isolation, they are generally not happy. This is where alcohol comes in.

A small quantity of alcohol may give a depressed person a slight boost in happiness. Unfortunately, alcohol itself is a depressive. So drinking more alcohol leads to feeling more depressed and more isolated.

Obviously, using alcohol to combat depression is self-defeating. Yet out of habit or custom or simply poor information many people drink more when they are depressed. I did it myself for a period many years ago.

It is not surprising that many suicides are accompanied by alcohol.

Reflection: Have you ever become sad and unhappy when your partner was drinking? Did you feel alone, even though he was there physically? What else did you feel?

Chapter 14
When Alcohol Abuse Is Not the Only Problem: The Issue of Dual Diagnosis

Is There Any Such Person as a Pure Alcoholic?

Does a functioning alcoholic exist who does not have at least one other mental disorder as defined by the *DSM-IV?* Does even a non-dependent alcohol abuser exist who does not have another mental disorder or serious psychological problem?

I doubt it in either case. Such a person could exist, but I'm not aware of ever having met one.

The Safest Assumption

It is probably safest to assume that there is always at least one other mental disorder or psychological problem present along with the alcohol abuse, whether or not it has progressed to alcohol dependence. The dual existence of alcohol problems and other psychological problems is the standard, not the exception.

Many professionals in alcohol addiction counseling and mental health counseling have failed to recognize the prevalence of dual disorders. This needs to change.

75

Slipping Through the Cracks

What happens in practice is disturbing. When I worked as the psychologist for a public mental health center, George came in for help with severe depression. He admitted to the intake worker that he also had an alcohol problem. since the center didn't treat addiction, the worker sent George to the public alcohol and drug counselling center. The intake counsellor recognized the depression and sent him back to the mental health center.

George was in poor emotional shape and gave up. He probably went back to the bottle. what we do know is that he never came back to either service. George might well have received the same response from many private therapists. I have seen this merry-go-round first hand numerous times.

The problem drinker, the functioning alcoholic or the derelict alcoholic are all real people seeking help with serious mental-health problems. Because of their mental health problems, they are fragile and don't have the will to fight for service. Instead, they slip through the cracks of a flawed health network, just like George did.

Bereavement, PTSD and Other Distress

Sometimes an emotional problem is commonly accepted as normal. An example is bereavement. Any of us who has been around long enough has experienced grief. Bereavement is listed in the **DSM-IV** as a short-term mental disorder (When it goes on too long, it is renamed *abnormal grieving*).

What if a woman is grieving because her partner died three months earlier? Since his death she has been getting increasingly depressed. Help would normally be readily available to her. However, if she finds herself drinking more and more heavily in reaction to the loss, she may have a much more difficult time finding the help she needs despite the fact that by this point she needs more help than ever.

When we look at the plight of a person with a more severe mental disorder such as Post Traumatic Stress Disorder (PTSD), the situation is even worse.

Unfortunately, the symptoms of PTSD are so disturbing that many people suffering with PTSD self-medicate with alcohol or other drugs. Huge numbers of people with PTSD go untreated. Many of these continue their alcohol abuse to the point of becoming addicted to alcohol.

The really sad part of is that PTSD can now be treated successfully with many of the modern energy psychology therapies.

I could go on with further examples. The point is that anxiety and unhappiness are symptomatic of a number of different mental disorders. The underlying emotional problem might be simply an adjustment problem, like a job loss, or it could be a severe mental disorder like bipolar disorder or schizophrenia.

Unhappy, distressed people frequently use alcohol to self-medicate just so they can feel a little better, or at least feel a little less pain. By the time they seek help for their mental/ emotional problem, they are often abusing alcohol. Because of their alcohol abuse, many are excluded from the treatment they need.

Hope

The good news is that increasing numbers of psychologists, counselors and other therapists are able and willing to help people with alcohol abuse problems **and** other psychological problems at the same time.

This new attitude applies to alcohol and drug rehab centers too. There is great variation in how well treatment centers deal with the emotional and psychological problems that are factors in alcohol abuse, but increasing numbers of treatment centers have the capability. As an example, the Sunshine Coast Health Centre, where I work as the Consulting Psychologist, pays a great deal of attention to the inevitable mental health issues which clients present.

Part Three deals with the repercussions of your partner's alcohol abuse for you and others. Topics include the chaos of the alcoholic family, codependency, work and financial implications, and the effects on your children. The issue of dealing with parents and in-laws who abuse alcohol is discussed in **Chapter 25**.

The topic of dual diagnosis is raised again in **Part Five**, this time in the context of selecting rehab professionals and facilities.

How his drinking affects you is the topic of the next chapter.

Reflection: Is there any such person as a pure alcoholic, that is an alcoholic with no other mental disorder or serious psychological problem? What other possible problems do recognize in your partner? Does he recognize them? Lots of alcoholics do.

Part Three
How Are You
and Your Family
Affected by His Alcoholism?

Chapter 15
How Are You Affected by Your Partner's Alcoholism?

The Chaos of Alcohol Abuse

Just like the rest of us, **alcoholics tend to live in families**. They have spouses. They have children. They have parents. And everyone in the family is affected when alcohol usage progresses from use and occasional misuse to alcohol abuse.

Bad things begin to happen to you as an alcoholic's wife. If you have children, bad things begin to happen to them as well.

It doesn't matter whether or not his alcohol abuse has progressed to alcohol dependence and addiction. It doesn't matter whether your partner has become a full-blown functioning alcoholic, or just frequently abuses alcohol. What matters is the effect that his drinking is having on his family and on himself.

The family is almost always in chaos when one or both adults abuse alcohol. A family in chaos is unstable, unbalanced, unpredictable and unsafe.

Society loosely refers to such a family as an **alcoholic family**. If there are no children we refer to the relationship as an **alcoholic marriage**.

In an alcoholic family there is little consistency in the way the partners treat each other, treat their children or react with the outside world. No one within the family or in contact with the family really knows what to expect from one moment to the next. Moods shift like sand in the desert or waves on the ocean.

The Escalation

Typically in an alcoholic marriage you find yourself participating in a lot of arguing, justifying and blaming. His rants become more and more verbally and emotionally abusive. The abuse is usually worse while he is under the influence of alcohol.

If his emotionally abusive behavior is allowed to continue, he will probably at some point become physically abusive. The physical abuse begins with his smashing things in front of you. Then it may move on to a shove or a slap. It may escalate to choking and worse.

One study found that among domestic assault cases, three quarters involved a family member who was abusing alcohol.

His progression from arguing and criticizing to verbal abuse and then to violence and physical abuse is usually punctuated by a great deal of remorse and frequent apologies. He becomes so contrite and conciliatory and just plain nice to be around that you begin to believe there may be hope.

The apologies and other acts of making up usually come the day after the abusive behavior. Unfortunately the niceness is short-lived, because nothing much else has changed in his life.

Reality Sets In

Being treated abusively is only the beginning of your problems. You may suffer exhaustion, become physically ill, become mentally ill or start avoiding all normal social contacts. Your self-esteem plummets. You have feelings of self-pity or self-hatred. You sometimes feel you don't know which end is up.

If you have children, you may find yourself having to assume responsibility for all the roles of both parents as his drinking continues. And of course you will resent it. This isn't what you bargained for when you married him. The added responsibility and pressure lead to more arguing and turmoil, and even less consistency.

The Money Issue

Another issue that predictably arises in an alcoholic family is money. Sooner or later the purchase of alcohol for the drinker will take precedence over other things the family needs.

Sometimes it comes even ahead of food for your children. If you are participating with your partner in the alcohol abuse, neglect of the children is almost inevitable, whether or not you are conscious of it. More about your children below...

Although financial problems usually first occur through distorted priorities, an even larger financial problem looms. That will occur when he loses his job or his business fails. Serious alcohol abuse cannot continue in the long term without job loss or business failure. His denial of his drinking problem doesn't alter this stark reality.

And What Else Happens to the Children?

The consequences of parental alcohol abuse can be very destructive to children in the family. Children often suffer syptoms of low self-steem, guilt, depression, loneliness, feelings of helplessness, and fears of abandonment.

Young children may show their distress in the form of bedwetting, nightmares, excessive crying and no friends. They develop into adults with very poor self-images like their alcoholic parent.

School problems are frequent. Truancy and lying increase. One study found that almost a third of young women who didn't complete high school had grown up in families with alcoholic parents.

Parents who abuse alcohol are more likely to sexually abuse their children or fail to protect them from other child predators.

The increased prevalence of medical problems for children in alcoholic families is even more startling than it is for the adults.

A study conducted in Pennsylvania compared children in alcoholic families with children whose parents did not abuse alcohol. Children in families with parental alcohol abuse had 24% more in-inpatient hospital admissions, and stayed on average 29% longer in the hospital. Their average hospital costs were over a third more than for other children.

If we were to extend these statistics to all of the U.S. and Canada, it would mean that the added annual costs of children's hospital care because of parental alcohol abuse would be in the multi-billion-dollar range. This statistic is as tragic as it is staggering.

Other Problems in an Alcoholic Marriage

I've spoken of some of the potentially nasty effects on you and your family when your partner is a functioning alcoholic or heading that way. But let's not ignore the health effects on him—liver problems, malnutrition, brain damage, burned-out kidneys and stomach, and increased susceptibility to common infections. Chronic alcohol abuse also leads to sexual dysfunction.

Legal problems can arise for your family as a result of his alcohol abuse, including charges for impaired driving or DUI, charges for uttering threats and charges for spousal assault.

Let us not forget the potential **long-term** harm he could do if he gets behind the wheel when he has been drinking.

When I was sixteen and my younger brothers were thirteen and eleven, my mother was killed by a driver who had been drinking. We paid dearly for his self-indulgence.

Reflection: What have you aleady noticed about how your partner's continued drinking has affected you?

Further Reflection: How are your children affected? (If you don't have children, think about the children of your partner's drinking friends.)

Chapter 16
The Nightmare of Codependence: Are you in the Dance of Alcohol?

Over the years many people in alcoholic marriages have come to me for help. More often than not the couple has entered into what I refer to as the **Dance of Alcohol**.

If you and your partner have entered the dance, you are probably finding that life revolves around him and his drinking. In the dance you try to please and appease him and not upset him. You make excuses for him and his drinking. You manage and protect the children in relation to him.

You resent what he is doing to your marriage and you blame him for it. He in turn blames you for making him drink. You may blame him for not exercising more control.

Sometimes you even agree to call his employer to claim he is sick, when really he just has a hangover. You get angry with yourself for doing it.

As the dance continues, self-esteem gets lower and lower for both of you as well as your children. And the lower your self-esteem, the more uncertainty and chaos there is for you and everyone else in your family.

What is happening to you in this situation is that you are becoming addicted to your partner's rescue and care.

If his life is about alcohol, yours is about looking after an alcoholic.

You can't back away from your addiction any easier than he can back away from his. Your attempts at not rescuing him are fraught with guilt and shame. Just as he reverts to drinking after yet another failed attempt to quit, you are quickly back to doing what you do best, devoting yourself to the rescue and care of an alcoholic.

You go round and round in what seems like a never-ending dance. You see no way out. You are dancing the dance of alcohol.

The Psychology of the Dance

Before trying to explain what is happening psychologically, let's take a detour back to your first years of life. When you were a toddler, you could not distinguish between yourself and other people. In fact you were psychologically merged with your mother.

In infancy you were totally dependent on your mother. But it may surprise you to know that your mother was also emotionally dependent on you. As human beings such mutual dependence is hard-wired into us to assure the survival of our helpless infants, thereby assuring the survival of the human species.

If it is not obvious to you how a mother is dependent on her infant child, let me ask you this. Have you ever known a mother whose young child has died?

What you probably observed went far beyond the expected level of grief over losing someone she cared about. **It was as if a part of herself had died.** When the child died, part of the mother died. And many a good marriage has failed under the stress of a child's death. That is the extent to which mother and child were merged.

As you grew up, you became increasingly aware that you were separate from your parents. By age nine or ten you began to understand that you were not the cause of parental behavior and moods.

Now, let's go back to the question about what is happening psychologically when you are in **the dance**.

What is happening is that you and your partner have merged identities. The popular name for this is codependence. Technically, it is *symbiosis*, but it doesn't really matter what it is called.

Maintaining a clear sense of self is incompatible with addiction and codependency. A clear sense of self is what prevents a slide into codependency.

Some critics of the concept of codependency confuse it with loving care. Codependency is different from mutual dependence, because two people can be mutually dependent and still have quite separate identities. True loving care is difficult in a codependent relationship. Love can be truer and deeper without codependence.

Codependency is Full of Opposites

Codependency is full of opposites. You have an intense pull towards your partner. You lose yourself in the intensity of the need to care for him. On the other hand you have a strong need to pull away and get a life for yourself. You may have left and come back, and then left again and come back again. There seems to be no middle ground. It's either total enmeshment or complete cutoff.

What is not well understood is that the cutoff is just as much a part of codependency as the enmeshment. Distancing yourself from your alcoholic spouse will not cure your addiction to his rescue and care. You are still overcompensating for his under-functioning.

Similarly, for the alcoholic, compulsive drinking and compulsive abstinence are two sides of the same coin. Compulsive abstinence does not "cure" the addiction to alcohol.

What is the effect of your codependency on your under-functioning, alcoholic partner? To put it bluntly, he stays stuck in his alcohol abuse. When you are there and enmeshed with him, he has no incentive to change. When you distance yourself, he declares his undying love and hints at cleaning up. Nothing really changes, nor can it change, as long as you continue to overcompensate for his shortcomings.

What is of paramount importance is that you recognize codependence. It is less important that you understand the psychological intricacies of how codependence develops.

Staying Together No Matter What

Isn't it curious how so many unhappy, codependent, alcoholic marriages last and last and last?

The ending of any marriage is traumatic, because it represents a huge loss. An ending represents a loss of hopes and dreams and expectations and beliefs. No matter how bad the marriage was, and no matter how it ended, its end still means the loss of an intimate partner.

The problem is that the experience of loss seems to be greater in the collapse of an alcoholic codependent marriage than it is in other marriage endings. With the merging of identities in codependence, separation feels like the death of part of yourself. Separation means the loss of part of your own identity.

Because of this double whammy, many alcoholic codependent couples get back together repeatedly to escape those awful feelings that a part of themselves is dying.

Are You Part of the Cause?

My final comment on what is happening is this: If your partner is abusing alcohol and you are part of the codependent, alcoholic dance, you are contributing to his continuing to drink. Nothing will change for the better while the dance continues. It can only get worse.

The dance is the glue that holds the alcohol abuse in place.

In Chapters 22, 23, and 24 we discuss strategies for releasing the hold that codependence has over you.

If you are in the dance of alcohol, you have become_____to your partner's rescue and care.

Reflection: How have you fed into his alcoholism and perhaps even contributed to it? [Make a list on a separate page of your notebook. Keep it nearby so you can add to it as you read on.]

Chapter 17
Your Partner
Is Still Working
or Running His Business...

C hronic alcohol abuse often leads to job loss or business failure. If your partner is chronically abusing alcohol, it is important that you understand what is going on at his workplace.

I've written this chapter in an attempt to make it very clear that the alcoholic leaves a path of destruction and liability far beyond his home environment. Alcohol abuse has a huge economic cost.

Your partner will not tell you about what is happening at work, because along with his alcohol abuse comes heavy denial and a tendency to minimize problems. His protesting that he is a "functioning alcoholic" is part of his delusional thinking.

Usually his employer first notices his absenteeism. He is away sick a lot, often a half day at a time. (You will likely be unaware of how frequently he is absent.) His employer will also find that your partner is often late for work, but always with a good explanation.

Your partner will blame others for his mistakes, and make excuses for his part in things that don't go well. He may occasionally have emotional outbursts with his coworkers, and his coworkers will begin to complain about his moods.

If your partner's job brings him in contact with the public, customers will shrink from that unmistakable alcoholic smell (even when he's not actually drinking) and drift away. Some may complain, but most won't. No one will ever say anything directly to him.

Without anyone really being aware of it at first, your partner's work may deteriorate from good to marginally satisfactory, and then to poor. Of course he will be able to argue his case with a range of reasons for his drop in performance.

Eventually alcohol use enters the workplace, usually starting with drinking on lunch breaks. If his job involves driving or running equipment, he could cause an accident.

If your alcohol-abusing partner is the employer rather than the employee, the economic risks are even more severe. There is a reasonable probability that if his alcohol abuse goes unchecked, his business will fail. That leaves customers, creditors and employees stranded.

His business failing could also leave you stranded. As an employer he probably will be ineligible for unemployment benefits. This of course depends on the jurisdiction in which you live. Be aware of what the risk is in your locale.

How your partner's employer may choose to deal or not deal with the alcohol abuse is the subject of a further chapter in **Part Four**.

Reflection: Have you already had hints that his job or business may be at risk. What signs have you noticed?

Chapter 18
The Adult Child
of an Alcoholic Parent

A detailed discussion of adult children of alcoholics is not called for here because so much information is available elsewhere. Rather, I will highlight a few of the possible results of either you or your partner growing up in an alcoholic family. I will also briefly talk about what can happen if one of your parents is still abusing alcohol.

Case One: He Grew Up in an Alcoholic Family.

These are some of the effects:

- Your partner probably grew up in **chaos**, so chaos seems normal.

- If he is typical of adult children of alcoholics, he suffers from **chronic unhappiness**.

- It will probably be particularly easy for him to **lie** whenever it suits his purpose.

- He will probably be adamant about keeping **family secrets.** He would have learned this lesson well in an alcoholic family.

- Your partner maintains an unusually **emotionally dependent** relationship with his parents.

- Even though he is a middle-aged adult, your partner desperately seeks **parental approval**. You find the hold his parents maintain over him to be particularly frustrating. It is as if he has not grown up and left home.

- If he isn't seeking parental approval, he may be exceptionally **hostile towards his parents**. He is like the defiant teenager who wants to leave home but can't. Either way, the parents have a hold on him.

Case Two: You Grew Up in an Alcoholic Family.

You grew up in an alcoholic family and have made a conscious decision either not to drink at all or never to let your occasional drink become problem drinking.

These are the possible outcomes:

- When you were growing up, your participation in the alcoholic dance seemed normal, and it was unavoidable anyway. The chances are high that you are deeply entangled in the alcoholic dance again.

- It seems natural for you to continue the childhood codependent pattern in your marriage, particularly if your partner abuses alcohol.

- Undoubtedly your growing up in an alcoholic family was an important factor in attracting and being attracted to the man who became your partner.

- Because of your beginnings, you will be much more likely to try to hold onto your own alcoholic marriage than you would be if you had grown up in a non-codependent family.

Case Three: At Least One of Your Parents Still Abuses Alcohol.

This could be your mom or dad, or your partner's mom or dad.

These are the typical effects:

- You experience a great deal of parental interference. You try to be nice, but you have to be very careful to maintain boundaries, lest Grandma take over the children.

- There may be a lot of parental volatility.

- There may be not-so-subtle attempts to split up your marriage.

- There may be threats or even attempts to take your children away.

- You may find out that the parents were driving under the influence alcohol while your children were in their care.

- You may eventually have to keep the parents away from your family. This of course would deprive your children of their grandparents. It would take great resolve on your part to do this, but the alternative of putting your children at risk may be unacceptable.

- Finally, you and your partner may have to face premature parental death. Suicide risk increases among older people, and triples when they are under the influence of alcohol.

Reflection: If either of you grew up around alcoholism, count the number of points in this chapter that apply to you and your family at present. Which ones surprised you?

Part Four
How to Help Yourself While Living with and Helping a Functioning Alcoholic

Introduction to Part Four

Parts **Two** and **Three** of Living with a Functioning Alcoholic dealt with various aspects of alcoholism and prob lem drinking—what it is, what causes it, what its effects are, and in particular, what its effects on you are.

Part Four deals with the nuts and bolts of what you can do, what you need to do and what you must avoid. Specifically, **Part Four** is aimed at helping you, the spouse of the problem drinker,

- to regain or to maintain your own sense of well-being,
- to cope with your partner's drinking,
- to avoid enabling his drinking and related problem behaviors, and
- to help him with his problem drinking when appropriate.

The next few chapters are about helping him. Then the topic shifts to how to help yourself to grow and to heal within your situation.

Caution: If there is any violence present, or if you are already in the process of leaving for whatever reason, skip to **Chapter 24: When to Pull the Plug on an Alcoholic Marriage.** Read it before anything else in **Part Four**.

Part Four ends with a short chapter on dealing with an alcoholic son or daughter or parent.

Chapter 19
What Not to Do
to Help Your Functioning
Alcoholic Partner to Heal:
Could You Be Making
Things Worse?

F irst and foremost after safety issues, consider whether you are part of the alcoholic dance. Ask yourself, "Have I entered the alcoholic dance?"

If you are not in the dance, this chapter will help you focus on the traps you must avoid.

If you are already in the dance, your primary job is to halt the damage by getting out of the dance. It is much easier said than done, but read on—there is hope.

Unless you get out and stay out of the dance, you can have little positive effect either on your partner's drinking problem or on your own pain. The problem is that staying in the dance enables your partner to continue abusing alcohol. It also enables him to continue with all the unwanted behaviors that flow towards you and your children.

Consequently, this chapter focuses on the things you should not be doing because they

- enable your partner's drinking, and
- keep you in the dance.

Don't be discouraged if some of my suggestions sound too hard to follow through on. Some of them may be difficult, especially if you have been in an alcoholic codependent relationship for a long time. But nothing is impossible.

Don't try to accomplish everything at once. Keep the list in front of you. Use each item as a gauge of how well you are doing. You can use these difficult-to-stop behaviors as indicators of your progress in getting out of the alcoholic dance.

What Not to Do to Help Your Alcohol-Abusing Partner

1. Do not accept blame or responsibility for his drinking. Multitudes of women less capable, less loving and less committed than you have partners without drinking problems.

2. Don't drink with him. He takes that as an affirmation that his alcohol abuse is OK.

3. Don't buy him alcohol. It is a vote of support.

4. Don't hide his alcohol or pour it out. That just makes it your problem instead of his.

5. Don't go to the bar to bring him home when he's drunk. Rescuing him enables him to avoid responsibility for the consequences of his drinking. He has to learn to take responsibility if things are ever going to change.

6. Don't criticize him for his drinking. Again, the message he gets is that it is your problem.

7. Don't participate in arguments when he's drinking or suffering the effects of drinking. It is pointless. The alcohol has taken away his ability to be rational, but not his ability to bully, control, be vindictive or to turn his problem into your problem.

8. Don't buy into his excuses for drinking. You know they are part of his delusional thinking, so don't even go there.

9. Don't accept his denial that he has a drinking problem. Denial that the earth is round has never made it flat.

10. Avoid using the label "alcoholic." That is like waving a red flag in front of a bull. What matters is how he treats you, the children, himself, his work and everyone else, not what label he carries. It's OK for him to call himself an alcoholic or functioning alcoholic; it's just not OK for you to do it when speaking to him.

11. Do not accept his apologies for raging, driving while under the influence, yelling at the kids, spending the grocery money on booze, ruining a holiday, or any other form of abuse. If he tries to apologize and get your sympathy and forgiveness, simply tell him that his bad behavior must stop.

12. Don't buy into the practice of keeping family secrets. If he has a drinking problem, do not try to hide it from friends or family. He may rage at your talking with others about his behavior or the difficulty you are having with it. But so what—he rages anyway.

13. Do not encourage your children to keep family secrets. Like you, they need to know they are free to just be. They are not responsible for their dad's problems. Good mental health is built on openness, not secrecy.

14. Do not deny or rationalize your partner's increasing alcohol dependence. Other people too have job pressures, family problems, money problems or health issues, but they don't turn to alcohol.

15. Do not use his drinking as an excuse for you to vent your anger. Of course you're angry. But venting it on him only helps him to justify his continuing alcohol abuse. He may even try to pick a fight with you to push you into the trap.

Each of the above actions you are presently engaged in is a sign you are involved in the alcoholic dance. You need to become more aware of what you are doing and not doing. If you are doing quite a few of the "do-not-do" things, you are probably deep in the dance.

Nevertheless, if you want things to change, the starting point is with you, one change at a time.

You are not to blame and you are not responsible for his behavior. In the final analysis, you are responsible for your own behavior, not his. Never forget this!

Only *he* is responsible for his drinking and his other behavior, no matter whom he tries to blame.

Reflection: Which ones on the "do-not-do" list surprised you?

Further Reflection: How deeply are you into the dance?

Even Further Reflection: What one or two on the list will you change first? When?

Chapter 20
What Steps Can You Take to Help Your Functioning Alcoholic Partner to Heal?

The discussion in the previous chapter centered on what to avoid if you want to help your partner stop abusing alcohol. Helping him means helping him to heal and grow beyond his need to self-medicate with alcohol.

This chapter focuses on positive things you can do to help him heal. There are three lists:

1. The first is a list of steps requiring simply that he be sober when you speak with him.

2. The second is a list of steps in preparation for the day when he admits he is aware of his drinking problem, or even that he needs help.

3. The third is the list of steps you need to take right now, for you. The third list is the most important.

Actions to Take Only When He Is Sober

1. When he is sober, tell him how you feel when he is drinking. This isn't criticism; it's just information he can take in only when he is sober.

2. Calmly tell him how afraid you were last night when he was drunk.

3. Tell him about the anger you feel when you see your life passing by. It may be anger at yourself, but he needs to know about it.

4. This is the time to tell him that the children are afraid of him when he is drinking.

5. If his drinking is a prelude to abusive or otherwise bad behavior, tell him when he is sober that his bad behavior must stop.

Actions to Prepare for the Day When He Admits He Has a Drinking Problem and Possibly Needs Help

1. By all means talk with your doctor about his drinking, even if your partner orders you not to.

2. Have the phone numbers handy, as well as meeting times and locations, of local AA or Life Ring chapters, should he ever ask for help. (chapters 29 and 31)

3. Become familiar with what local alcohol and drug counseling services are available. Have phone numbers handy.

4. Check out what the closest detoxification facilities are. Again have the phone number handy. (Chapter 28)

5. Know what treatment facilities are available within your geographic region and beyond. (Chapter 32)

6. Find out which local private therapists have expertise and experience in helping people with alcohol problems, whether the problem drinking is occasional misuse or serious addiction. Make some phone calls. (Chapter 33)

7.   Understand that his stopping drinking is only the first step in his recovery.

Actions to Take for Yourself, Beginning Right Now

As with any personal healing, awareness is the crucial first step. It follows then that a number of the actions I suggest you take are simply invitations to observe yourself with love and curiosity. There is no need for self-criticism. You probably get far too much criticism already.

I suggest that you get help if you need it. Although professional help may be required in some instances, there are often sources of help available free for the asking. Your first move is to evaluate how well you are handling each point on your own.

Chapter 21 goes into more detail about how to put some of these self-help suggestions into practice.

Here is your self-help list:

1.   Accept the reality that your partner's continued alcohol abuse may lead to increasing marital discord, probable violence and possibly a painful separation. This is a tough reality to accept without sparking your terror of it all ending. But the necessary first step is awareness and acceptance of what is.

2.   Find support for yourself as you disentangle yourself from the dance.

3.   Discuss his drinking with your friends. You may find couple of them are also dealing with problem drinking in their families. You can be important supports to one another. You might even organize a discussion group based on **Living with a Functioning Alcoholic.**

4. Pursue your own independent interests. If you don't have any, develop some. Take a class, join a church group, or start a home-based business, but do something that is yours. Don't ask permission; just do it and then tell him what you have done.

5. Pursue your own personal growth. Growth happens anyway: you are far beyond where you were ten years ago. When you make your growth conscious and deliberate, you get better and happier faster.

6. Protect your children. First, keep them safe. Be as consistent as possible with them. If they have a stable loving alternative place they can be, like with grandparents or an aunt and uncle, then let them spend time there often.

7. Recognize that ongoing alcohol abuse in your family will severely limit your children's social development, education, ability to form good relationships as adults, and generally lessen their chances of success in life. This is the general pattern, so do whatever you need to do to make your family the exception. See Number 6 above.

8. Above all, make your own mental, physical and spiritual health your number one priority.

9. Get help for yourself, especially if you can't shake the belief that you are somehow responsible for your partner's drinking.

10. Get help for yourself, if you need to become more conscious of how **your actions may be contributing** to his continued alcohol abuse.

11. Get help for yourself, so you can become more conscious of how **your needs may be contributing** to his continued alcohol abuse.

    - Do you care too much?

    - Do you need someone to rescue?

    - Are you terrified of being alone?

12. Get help for yourself if you feel shame or guilt, or that you somehow deserve abuse. Shame and guilt can't help you, and no one ever deserves abuse. That includes you!

_____is the crucial first step in healing.

Reflection: How far along are you in your discussions with your partner about how his drinking effects you?

Further Reflection: How do your friends respond when you tell them about your concerns with his drinking?

Chapter 21
The Slippery Slope Towards Becoming Unemployable: Is Your Partner's Job at Risk?

Chapter 17 dealt with the subject of how alcohol abuse can lead to deterioration in job performance, sometimes with severe economic consequences.

This chapter takes the subject further. It discusses the options, should an employer want to help your partner with his drinking problem.

Having a better picture of what your partner's employer could be thinking and doing may help you support your partner in getting help. He may be still in heavy denial that he has any problem, but you need to be ready if he gets a nudge from his employer.

As explained earlier, an alcohol problem usually shows up in the workplace first in a pattern of absenteeism, lateness for work, and generally deteriorating reliability. Whether or not he is actually drinking at work, he may be having increasing difficulties in getting along with his coworkers and/or bosses.

But usually the alcohol eventually enters the workplace. Alcohol is frequently implicated in worksite accidents and poor relationships with coworkers, customers, and management.

The Employee as a Valuable Asset

It doesn't matter whether your partner works in an industrial company, a professional office, a government department, a school or a retail store. In all cases a good employer looks at its employees as assets and watches those assets carefully. If the employer suspects that the employee/ asset has a drinking problem, action is essential.

It is almost inevitable that without intervention the employee will eventually become a liability to the employer— a risk of injuring himself, a risk to other employees, a risk to employee morale, a legal liability and a public-relations liability.

If the drinking has been going on for some time, the employer may have already entered incident reports in your partner's file. A warning may have been given. Counseling may have been offered. Some companies will even offer to send a key employee to an expensive alcohol rehab center for a month.

What the employer is trying to do is tell your partner that there are consequences to his drinking. The endpoint of continued inaction is dismissal from the job with cause.

A good employer never overlooks the problem. A good employer always takes action before the employee/asset becomes a serious liability.

With some early confrontation and intervention by the employer, the employee might well clean up his act and get back on track. This could be the nudge your partner needs.

If he never gets that nudge, or if he gets the nudge but ignores it, he may find himself living as an unemployed, broken man that nobody wants to hire.

I have seen it happen. It is sad to see a formerly active, competent, contributing man sink into the personal degradation of being unemployable and feeling useless.

Brad and I met in graduate school. He was married and had a couple of small children. Things were not well on the home front and he was drinking. He was also taking medication for an illness.

After graduation he managed to find a one-year contract position, but was disappointed he did not get a continuing professional position. This was very troubling to him and he drank more. He fulfilled his contract, but it was not renewed.

Between his drinking and the devastation of not being able to find a new position, he and his wife separated. He had no place to go, and about a month later he was found dead in his car. The alcohol in combination with the medication had killed him. He was thirty-two.

Reflection: What signs (if any) have there been of problems in the workplace for your partner?

Chapter 22
How to Regain and Keep Your Sense of Well-Being and Self-Esteem

This chapter brings the focus back to you, where it belongs. Remember the piece of wisdom,

**"For things to change,
First I must change."**

This is as true when living with an alcoholic as it is anywhere else in life. In your situation it is probably even more crucial, because your partner is stuck in his drinking and probably will not initiate change. It really is up to you if things are to change.

The focus of this chapter is on you, because you may have already tried and failed many times to change him.

Would you like to have a framework for self-healing and some tools you can use right away—today? While reading this chapter, just keep an open mind and let the ideas sink in.

The only thing that could stand in the way of your getting some immediate results is simply not trying them.

Unfortunately, it is a lot harder to teach people how to help themselves than to teach people how to help others. Nevertheless, this chapter and the following two are aimed at helping you to help yourself. You may need to review this chapter a few times before you get the full impact.

- The **good news** is that once you get the hang of it, you can do a great deal of self-healing without the assistance of a healing professional.

- The **bad news** is that it is hard for most people to believe that is possible.

- The **good news** is that you can overcome any of your limiting beliefs if you are open to doing so and really want to.

How Strong Is Your Intention?

All self-healing and self-growth begins with intention. Without intention, nothing much changes. If you are wavering, just ask the question you have asked yourself a hundred times: "How long can I go on like this?" If your answer is less than "for the rest of my life," then use your answer to help you resolve to change as you learn how.

If a problem drinker is sent to rehab against his will, there is little chance he will deal with his drinking problem and the underlying issues. On the other hand, if he goes to a treatment center because he has a strong intention to deal with his alcohol problem, his probability of success is many times higher.

The same thing applies to you. If you are enmeshed in the dance with a problem drinker, your strong intention to change yourself is critical to your getting out of the dance.

Take Care of Yourself First

The reason your self-esteem is low and you do not have much sense of wellbeing is because you have not been putting yourself first. You have been trying to take care of everyone else. You have put your own needs last so many times that it feels normal. (Actually, it is "normal" in a dysfunctional family, but isn't that what you want to change?)

The first thing you need to do is set a strong intention to take care of yourself first.

You may balk at the notion of putting yourself first, because on the surface it may seem selfish. But if you don't take care of yourself first, you won't be much good to anyone else.

The great healers have all made personal self-care a top priority.

If you are in the alcoholic dance, you have not been taking adequate care of yourself. If you are in an alcoholic codependent relationship, and you want to take care of yourself, then set your intention to get out of the dance.

Inspired Action in the World

So... you have set a strong intention to take care of yourself first and to get out of the dance. What's next?

The next step is to take action. And the more inspired your actions the better!

In **Chapter 19** you examined an extensive **list of things not to do** with regard to living with a functioning alcoholic or alcohol abuser. In **Chapter 20** you examined a **list of things to do** with regard to living with a functioing alcoholic. While holding your intention to take care of yourself first, start right away to act on those do's and don'ts.

Read them again. Copy them out and put them where you can refer to them regularly.

If you feel yourself faltering, remember your intention to get out of the dance.

Of course you may falter sometimes. That's okay and it's expected. You are human. Simply give yourself a loving hug, return to your intention and calmly move forward.

Give Yourself a Life!

As you create a life for yourself, you will reestablish your self-esteem and sense of well being.

You used to have a life, but then you merged your identity with your partner. Now is the time to rebuild your life. Now is the time to pursue your individual passions and interests.

But what if your self-esteem is so low that you don't think you have any interests? The answer is not complicated. Simply set your intention to develop some interests that are your own and take action anyway.

Actions can be anything. Join a self-help group. Make some new friends. Join an art class. Read a self-help book. Volunteer. Go to the gym. Get self-help tapes and play them while driving your car. Join a walking group. Get a job, or a new job. Go to church.

Find some other women whose partners are problem drinkers. They are everywhere. Then start a discussion group using **Living with a Functioning Alcoholic** as your focus. The possibilities are endless.

If you have a clear intention to develop some personal, outside interests, and you take action, it won't be long before your life includes one or more activities or pursuits that you are really excited about. That is the inevitable result of having a clear intention and taking inspired action.

Setting your intention and taking deliberate, inspired action sends a message to the universe that you are changing. It is almost inevitable your self-esteem will soar from where it was.

The above examples are all about taking action in the external world. But besides such important external actions, you will need to take some definitive internal action.

Inspired Action Within

If something goes wrong with your computer, you may joke about the cyber gods conspiring against you, but you call somebody to come and correct the programming. Most of the time the programming is fine, but when it isn't, you recognize the problem by the results you are getting.

Like computers, people work from their programming too. Much of what we do is automatic. Much of what we think and feel is automatic as well. Our actions and thoughts are supported by an elaborate system of beliefs, mostly unconscious and mostly internalized early in life. This is our programming.

Why is it that when people are not getting the results they want, they don't immediately check out their programming? Instead, they speak of bad luck, lacking money, lacking good genes, being too old, being married to the wrong person, lacking education, living in a poor economy, lacking power or lacking intelligence.

In short, people tend to blame external conditions and other people when things are not working. Suggesting their programming might be the problem makes them defensive: they mumble something about not being able to change because that's just the way they are.

If you look back over your life, you will recognize lots of beliefs that you held earlier but no longer do. Beliefs that once served you—resourceful beliefs—no longer do. They have become unresourceful. In discarding the unresourceful beliefs of earlier years you have simply corrected your programming. We continue to correct our programming throughout life, whether or not we intend to.

We can intentionally correct our programming by embarking on a "belief watch," a deliberate attempt to be ever more aware of what beliefs are operating when we are not getting the results we want.

Beliefs can be about anything, but we can easily recognize a lot of belief statements by the way they begin:

I am..., I can't..., I'm supposed to..., I'm afraid of..., Everybody..., Nobody..., Marriage is..., Men are..., Women are..., I deserve..., I don't deserve..., He deserves..., He can't..., He won't..., He would never..., Life is...

Beliefs are simply internal statements that guide us through life. They may be resourceful beliefs that help us get the results we want. Or they may be unresourceful beliefs that block the achievement of our desired results.

Belief, as I am using the term here, is not about **The Truth**, but about your personal truth at a point in time. For every belief one person holds to be true, someone else holds the opposite to be true.

What I am suggesting is that watching for and replacing unresourceful beliefs, beliefs that no longer serve you, is the inspired action within that you need to take as part of your self care.

To better understand this point, pretend you are at an impasse over some issue with your partner. You are wondering what to do to get unstuck.

You intentionally engage your **belief watch**: You stand back and look at the whole situation to see if you are carrying any unresourceful beliefs into your argument.

Your belief watch could suggest, for example, that you have a belief that your partner is going to dump you.

As if that isn't bad enough, you realize that for most of your life you have been carrying an underlying belief that everyone abandons you, and another irrational belief that you can't survive on your own.

It must be pretty obvious that operating from any of the beliefs I just described can't help you. Let's take a closer look.

1.   The belief that your partner is going to abandon you doesn't help you. It could be true or it could be false. But if it is a belief filled with fear it will hamper your ability to function.

2.   An underlying belief that everyone abandons you can only harm you. If that is what you believe, that is what you will see in many situations. You have probably attracted into your life the sort of people who would abandon you. A belief that you will be abandoned can only interfere with your enjoyment of life. Unconsciously holding such a belief inevitably leaves you stuck.

3.   A belief that you can't survive on your own is also very limiting. You may not know how, but you will survive. This belief leaves you stuck in fear with every disagreement you have with your spouse.

Millions of women have learned to survive alone. And since you have taken the initiative to read **Living with a Functioning Alcoholic**, you are already stronger than most of them.

There is more in the next chapter about inspired internal action. But for now, just becoming more aware of the beliefs that limit you will be a giant step. In fact, you will look back at this time as an inspired leap.

Be Gentle with Yourself When You Get Stuck

Being stuck can take many forms:

- There may be something negative in your life and you simply can't get your mind off it. That's worry.

- You could be trying to change something in yourself, and can't figure out why you're not making progress.

- You may find there is a circumstance that triggers you to overreact, and no matter what you try, you can't seem to avoid being triggered.

- Perhaps you hold an unresourceful belief you just can't seem to shake, like, "I'm going to end up as a bag lady."

Since personal healing and personal growth are lifelong pursuits, it is almost inevitable that you will occasionally find yourself stuck. Maybe you will even get stuck frequently in the early stages of trying to get out of the dance.

Just be gentle with yourself. Remind yourself that everyone gets stuck, and everyone has the capacity to get through difficult times and situations if their intention is strong.

The subject of the next chapter is what to do when you can't seem to figure out how to get unstuck.

Reflection: How strong is your intention to change? Are you ready to take inspired action within and without?

Chapter 23
Do You Need the Self-Help Power Therapies?

What can you do when you find yourself stuck in an unresourceful belief, a belief you just cannot seem to let go of? What can you do about a trigger that just won't go away? What can you do when you feel yourself stuck in powerlessness?

First, **forgive yourself and accept yourself as you are**, even though you seem to be holding onto something you don't want to be holding onto. Remember, it has probably been there for most of your life and has become quite entrenched.

You could go to see a good psychologist and receive help to get unstuck quickly. Many people do.

As a professional psychologist I use a number of therapeutic procedures to help people release unresourceful beliefs and habits. Clients do get unstuck.

I too am human and I sometimes get stuck. I use the same procedures on myself that I use with clients. I have a series of methods I turn to whenever I need to release something. Every self-help procedure I teach clients I have tested on myself.

You too can learn how to use the self-help power therapies.

125

The Self-Help Power Therapies

There are many different therapeutic procedures available that can help you release an unresourceful belief and replace it with a resourceful one. They also work for releasing unwanted fears, upsets, habits and cravings.

At the core of most such procedures is a common element. Instead of avoiding or denying a belief or behavior, they encourage you to face the emotion that surrounds that belief or behavior. Let yourself feel it. Let yourself be in it. And then release it. These therapies provide a variety of ways of accomplishing the last part, releasing the energy.

In the balance of this chapter I will briefly describe several powerful therapeutic procedures that are easy to learn and use on your own. People who use any of these over time are often profoundly successful in their self-healing and growth.

Again, I am the guinea pig. There is nothing in the remainder of this chapter that I have not applied repeatedly and successfully in my own healing and growth.

First I discuss the **Sedona Method**, because it is elegant in its simplicity. Then I go on to discuss several Energy Psychology healing approaches.

With each method discussed, further materials and training can be accessed through www.neillneill.com/recommended-resources/. Think of this chapter as your gateway to some of the best self-help tools available.

I recommend you read the whole chapter to get an overview of the range of tools available. Then check out some of the links at www.neillneill.com/recommended-resources/.

The Sedona Method

Although the **Sedona method** has a number of variations and sub-procedures, the basic protocol is very simple.

- First, **get into the emotion** that surrounds a belief, an event, a person or an expectation where you find yourself stuck.

- Then ask yourself, **"Could I let this feeling go?"** Allow an answer to come. Regardless of whether your answer is 'yes' or 'no'...

- Ask yourself, **"Would I be willing to let this go?"** Allow an answer to come. Regardless of whether your answer is 'yes' or 'no'...

- Ask yourself, **"When?"** Allow an answer to come.

- If there is any emotion left, repeat the procedure with the three questions until the emotion around the belief, event, person, or expectation is gone.

Most of the time, you will experience an internal shift. If you look back on what you did a few hours later, you will notice your feelings around the issue are less intense or even gone.

I know you are thinking nothing that simple could possibly work. And I can't blame you. That was my first reaction too. But let me tell you a story about Lester Levinson, the founder of the Sedona Method.

In 1952 Lester was forty-two years old and a successful physicist-engineer, but an unhappy man with a lot of health problems. After his second coronary the doctors sent him home to die.

Instead of dying as expected, he went inside himself to look for some answers. What he found was a way of letting go of all his internal limitations. He used it for three months.

Within the three months his body became totally healthy again and he found unshakable inner peace.

He lived until 1994. That was forty-two years after he was sent home to die at age forty-two. What he discovered became known as the **Sedona Method**[4].

Note: Lester Levinson is a superb example of the "inspired action within," as discussed in the previous chapter.

Training courses in the *Sedona Method* are available. A schedule of the training events is available on the Internet if you are interested.

However, you can readily learn the Sedona Method through a book, a set of training CDs and an excellent workbook. Everything you need is available on the Internet. See *The Sedona Method* at www.neillneill.com/recommended-resources/.

The Energy Psychology Healing Tools

Now I want to discuss a group of methods from energy psychology. Energy psychology is a broad field of study and healing. It involves working directly with your body's energy centers, energy flows and energy fields.

Energy centers, or *chakras*, are places on your body where there is a concentration of moving energy that becomes stuck when you are experiencing a negative emotion. Anyone who has practiced yoga knows about chakras.

Energy flows through a network of subtle energy paths called *energy meridians*. When you are in emotional trouble, energy becomes stuck in some of the junctions (nodes). Acupuncturists get the energy flowing by inserting needles into these nodes within the meridian system.

Your **energy field** or *aura* is the sheath of energy that surrounds your body. With negative emotion your energy field

---

[4] The Sedona Method is copyrighted and is reproduced with permission from the Sedona Training Associates.

may develop bumps, gaps and holes. A Reiki master, a Pranic Healer or a Healing Touch practitioner focuses on your energy field. Your chakras are very much involved too, because they show up in your aura.

There are many methods and variations of these methods within energy psychology. I have extensive training and experience in a number of them and hold the designation, **Diplomate, Comprehensive Energy Psychology**. But for present purposes I will limit discussion to two of my favorites.

Emotional Freedom Technique

One of my favorites is the **Emotional Freedom Technique**, commonly known as **EFT**. Gary Craig developed it, based on work by Dr. Roger Callahan. Gary Craig and his psychologist colleague, Dr. Pat Carrington, trained me.

I have selected EFT for inclusion in the chapter for three reasons.

1. I use it myself, both on myself and with my clients.

2. It is easy to learn and use, and it is very effective.

3. The information about EFT available on-line is among the best to date of any energy psychology methods.

At its very simplest, EFT involves tapping lightly with your fingers on points on your face, body and hands, while you are feeling the emotion surrounding a past event, a worry about the future, a person or an unresourceful belief.

EFT works on the energy flows within your body. You tap on the same energy points an acupuncturist might place a needle.

Your energy flows become stuck or blocked when you are experiencing a negative emotion. Tapping on certain points tends to release these stuck flows. As the energy flows are reestablished and balanced, the negative emotion tends to dissipate.

Simple? You bet! Effective? After clients have used EFT, they often use the word "miraculous."

Why not try EFT right now?

Are you ready to try a two-minute experiment?

1. Pick something that causes you to get anxious when you think about it. Focus on that.

2. Let yourself feel the anxiety.

3. Then while you are feeling the anxiety,

    - Tap a number of times gently just under one eye.

    - Then thump your fists gently on your collarbone spots. (These are the notches just below where your collarbone joins your breastbone.)

    - Go back and forth a few times tapping under your eye for a few seconds and then thumping on your collarbone spots for a few seconds, all the time continuing to think about what causes your anxiety.

Could you feel your anxiety dissipating? When I have tried this little demonstration during a public talk, usually about two thirds of the audience reports some reduction in anxiety. This is only a part of the EFT technique. There is much more to the full procedure, and of course the full procedure is more effective more of the time. But even this little bit can have a positive effect.

EFT has evolved over the past five years. Our understanding has evolved and deepened. The possibilities for use of EFT have greatly expanded. I wanted to find an EFT training package that met several criteria before I would recommend it to you for purchase. My criteria were:

- It had to be up-to-date.
- It had to be easy to use and learn from.
- It had to be concise.
- It had to be not overly expensive.

My conclusion is that Dr. Pat Carrington provides training materials that are concise, most up-to-date, easy to use and learn from, and affordable. You will be able to learn the basics within about an hour of starting. Her learning package consists of a two-DVD set with an ebook.

Dr. Carrington is an excellent teacher. She continues to do pioneering work in the evolution of EFT. I can recommend her without reservation.

Go to www.neillneill.com/recommended-resources/ to learn more about EFT, Dr. Carrington and her and her DVD training package and to order it.

As you get further into learning and using EFT, Gary Craig's website features many case examples of real people with real problems who were treated using EFT. He offers extensive DVD and print training materials. Go to www.neillneill.com/recommended-resources/.

As with the Sedona method, many people teach some version of EFT, and training workshops are widely available. If you want to travel, you could even take the training from one of the pioneers, Gary Craig or Dr. Pat Carrington. But with the quality of materials that are available on the Web, you don't have to wait.

The Tapas Acupressure Technique

Tapas Fleming, an acupuncturist, developed Tapas Acupressure Technique (TAT) in the 1990s in her work with allergies. It is an energy psychology technique that has turned out to have wide applicability. It is quite effective in its simplicity.

I have found TAT to be a very simple and unobtrusive method which can release a mountain of stress.

I learned TAT from Tapas herself in 2000, the same year I trained with Gary Craig. Now there are people worldwide who teach TAT. If you want to take a course, check out Tapas's own teaching schedule on her web site. However, as you will see below, traveling to a workshop isn't really necessary.

TAT involves holding the fingers of one hand and the palm of your other hand on your head in a particular way. The position is simply called "the pose." While you are holding the pose, you go through a series of seven simple steps in your thinking.

The pose is very easy to learn when you can see it done, but not so easy to explain in words. On Tapas's website you can watch a two-minute video for free. She will show you how to do the TAT pose. Go to www.neillneill.com/recommended-resources/.

You can also download for free the seven TAT steps and the basic manual. Other than possibly needing help with shedding your disbelief that anything so simple could work, that's all you need to get you started.

There are further training materials available for purchase through Tapas Fleming's website.

For the time being that's all I really want to say about the best self-help power therapies available. If you learn and use EFT, TAT, the Sedona Method or all three, and exercise a little patience and persistence, you should be able to get unstuck on most issues without professional help.

Do these techniques always work? There are some people who experience difficulty achieving success with one or another method on their own. And of those who generally do experience success, there may be some issues that they can't seem to budge on their own. But overall the results have been very positive for the majority of those who try the methods.

Seek Professional Help when You Need It

In spite of the excellence of EFT, TAT and the Sedona Method, you could still find yourself occasionally unable to get unstuck by yourself. Yes, that sometimes happens to me too. These are the times when it would be prudent to seek the help of an appropriate professional if at all possible. That's what I do.

Try to find a professional who is proficient in one or more of the energy psychology methods. In my experience, energy psychology methods tend to work much faster than traditional talk therapy and even standard cognitive behavior therapy. Because it is faster, it will probably cost you less.

Once you get unstuck, you can continue the work at home on your own.

Reflection: What other self-help tools do you already use. If they work for you, keep using them? (meditating, nature walking, journaling, prayer, singing, keeping a gratitude journal)

Chapter 24
When to Pull the Plug
on an Alcoholic Marriage

If your marriage has deteriorated to the point where you are questioning whether you should even continue to be with your alcoholic partner, **the first thing to consider is your safety.**

Make Safety Your First Priority

If your partner is seriously verbally abusing you or has ever physically abused you, you are in real danger. You need to get yourself to a safe place quickly. The urgency is tripled if you have children.

If the arguments, particularly the arguments around alcohol, have turned into verbal abuse and bullying when he is drinking, there is a high probability that his verbal abuse will eventually lead to physical abuse.

Mary said, "I know how to handle him." What she did not understand, or at least did not want to believe, is that no one can "handle" an intoxicated, irrational, angry man. Phil would punch walls and break furniture when he was angry, but had never hit her. She didn't leave him until after he had thrown her to the floor and choked her. She is lucky to still be able to take action. She and her children are now doing fine.

An abusive intoxicated man could be dangerous to anyone who crosses him. It often takes three or four police to subdue an angry, intoxicated man, and one of the police may get hurt in the process. What chance would you have?

No matter how much you love him, there is no justification for staying in a dangerous place. Nevertheless, plan your move carefully.

If you are in danger of violence while you are with him, you may be in more immediate danger after you leave him.

Women are most likely to be murdered by their partners after they leave. Access the resources in your community so that you can make the safest possible transition. Then go to a shelter. Do whatever you need to do, but get out and stay safe.

You are no good to anyone if you are dead. You are also no good to anyone if you stay so long your self-esteem is battered into nothingness.

After Becoming Clear...

The second possible reason for leaving your marriage is more complex; it involves a number of assumptions.

- You have been working on yourself.

- You have been successful in getting out of the dance of alcoholism.

- You have a strong intention to continue to grow mentally, emotionally, and spiritually.

- You have a strong intention to be your own person.

- You are no longer muddled, but are thinking clearly.

If these conditions describe you, this would be a good time to take stock of your marriage.

As you take stock of your life and your marriage, you may find that your partner has begun to take a look at his alcohol abuse and has begun to do something about it. You may find the conflict level to be much lower. This is all good and bodes well for the future.

However, you also might find that you simply cannot live with the man your partner is, and don't expect to ever be able to. Maybe you could once, but not anymore. In other words, you may find that in spite of the improvements in your marriage, you have moved on emotionally, mentally and spiritually.

You may decide that you simply do not want to spend your life with this person. You may decide you want more from your life, and you cannot do it while living with this man.

This may not be the outcome you intended when you embarked on your program of self growth. The outcome could have just as easily been a renewal of your marriage. Remember: change is unpredictable and irreversible. Your eyes were open when you decided to heal and grow.

Regardless of whether you decide to stay or decide to leave, you are in a much better position emotionally and mentally and spiritually to make your choice with the clarity and calm of your inner wisdom. With clear thinking you will also be better equipped to keep yourself safe.

When in Doubt...

My final comment is this: If you are safe, but are unsure about what to do, be patient and stay put. When things are moving forward on the self-care and self-growth front, time is still a great healer. Miracles do happen.

Reflection: How safe are you?

Chapter 25
How to Help
an Alcoholic Parent
or Adult Child

L*iving with a Functioning Alcoholic* could have been written without reference to alcoholic parents or adult alcoholic children. However, troubling family situations involving either alcoholic parents or alcoholic adult children are so prevalent that they are worth covering at least briefly.

If you are dealing with an alcoholic partner, you may well be dealing with an alcoholic parent or in-law too. Likewise, at some point you may be faced with dealing with an alcoholic son or daughter.

It is very disturbing to watch your parents deteriorating while one or both are abusing alcohol. It may be even more disturbing to watch one of your adult children destroying his or her life with alcohol abuse.

Our natural tendency is to try to rescue them, scold them, or both. **Neither works. Neither helps them. They never have.**

In fact, for either the alcoholic parent or the alcoholic offspring, the rescuing and scolding only enable them to continue with their alcohol abuse.

The single most important thing to remember about the alcoholic son, the alcoholic daughter, the alcoholic mother or the alcoholic father is that they are adults.

As adults they and they alone are responsible

for their lives. You are not!

Previous chapters have outlined various do's and don'ts of dealing with an alcoholic partner. Most of these suggestions are useable in dealing with an alcoholic parent or offspring, because the same principles apply.

As a responsible adult, your primary responsibility is to look after yourself. If you are in a marriage, you need to look after yourselves and your relationship. If you have dependent minor children, your primary responsibilities extend to them.

The Wedge Factor

It seems as if alcoholic parents and alcoholic offspring are programmed to drive wedges into your relationship. They interfere and meddle with your lives. They drain your strength. They may do it unconsciously, but they do it nevertheless.

Paying attention to all the do's and don'ts mentioned in **Chapters 19 and 20** will usually reduce the problem of their interfering with your primary family. But sometimes it becomes necessary to distance yourself from the alcohol-abusing son, daughter or parent.

You might ask, "How could this possibly help them?" The answer is simple. It helps by gently nudging them towards taking responsibility for their lives.

If you take responsibility for their emotional, physical and/or financial well-being, they won't learn to do it. It's as simple as that. And if you enable them to avoid taking responsibility now, how will they handle their lives when you can't be there to rescue them?

The Magnet of Grandchildren

The situation may be even more heart-wrenching when your grandchildren are involved. If your son or daughter or their spouse is abusing alcohol, you know without a doubt it is hurting your grandchildren. And of course you want to rescue your grandchildren.

But any attempts at rescue usually have the effect of enabling the alcohol abuse.

Your grandchildren may be growing up in a very unhealthy environment. But if your grandchildren are not being abused in a way that the authorities would recognize, don't interfere. If your grandchildren's parents are behaving badly enough to involve the authorities, then involve them. But don't intervene yourself.

There are a number of reasons why you personally should not intervene, but one stands out above the others.

Your children and their spouses may need your wisdom and experience at some point. Your grandchildren may sometime need to use your home as a safe haven. You cannot be fully available to your alcoholic son or daughter and to their children, if you have attempted to interfere with their lives, or if you have allowed them to interfere with yours.

Everything I've just said about dealing with adult children who abuse alcohol applies to parents who abuse alcohol. When your parents begin to fail, they may need to depend on you just to survive. If you have managed to avoid entangling yourself with them and their alcohol abuse, you will be able to help them with much less chance of your becoming resentful or their becoming bitter.

Reflection: How does ths chapter apply to you?

Part Five
Rehab Possibilities for the Functioning Alcoholic

Introduction to Part Five

The purpose of **Part Five** is to help you gain some basic understanding about treatment options and the risks that go with each. You need this knowledge for when and if he says he needs help.

Part Five is not about persuading you to adopt a particular route with regard to treatment for your partner. There are many options.

Having said that, it is important for you to understand that treatment can play a pivotal role in your partner's overcoming his problem drinking or recovering from his alcoholism.

In **Part Five,** I freely use the term "alcoholism" when explaining treatment options. Please understand that the treatment options are for anyone with a drinking problem, not just the person who has developed a full addiction to alcohol.

Chapter 26 begins with an explanation of why *Living with a Functioning Alcoholic: A Woman's Survival Guide* should include a substantial section on rehab. Most of the rest of the **chapter** deals with the economics of alcohol consumption, abuse and treatment.

Chapter 27 is about the issue of cure. Can alcoholism be cured or is it a lifelong condition? This is another one of those debates without end.

Chapter 28 is about detoxification services. Such services can greatly reduce the health risks to an alcoholic during the withdrawal process.

Chapters 29 and 30 are devoted to a discussion of Alcoholics Anonymous (AA), by far the most publicly-known, free, self-help resource for recovering problem drinkers.

Chapter 31 introduces a variety of less well-known self-help alternatives to AA and its twelve-step program. Recovery is not a one-size-fits-all process. There will be an approach that is uniquely suited to your partner's needs, should he decide he wants help.

Chapter 32 is devoted to alcohol (and drug) addiction treatment centers, both those based on the AA model and those following other recovery models.

Chapter 33 deals with individualized therapeutic programs for the problem drinker, an important alternative to the rehab center program. Your awareness of this option could be vital.

Chapter 34 summarizes the seven major things you should look for as you research rehab options for your partner.

Chapter 26
Rehab Options for
the Functioning Alcoholic:
An Overview

You might ask why ***Living with a Functioning Alcoholic - A Woman's Survival Guide*** would include a substantial section on alcohol rehab. There are two major reasons for **Part Five**:

1. First and foremost it is very important for anyone living with a functioning alcoholic in their home to be intimately familiar with what help available for him when he is ready.

2. You live in the presence of alcohol abuse. It is possible that you may have developed a drinking problem yourself. Perhaps your problem is not as bad as his, but it still could be a problem or could become one. Or perhaps you are in recovery yourself. Arm yourself with the necessary knowledge.

When your partner's alcohol abuse leads to consequences disturbing enough for him to think about quitting, **you need to be ready in the moment with good information**. You need to be ready when he brings up the subject, not a day or a week later.

Alcohol Economics 101

There are approximately two million clients in alcohol and drug treatment centers in the United States at any one time. The cost is typically around $10,000 per month, but sometimes it is double that.

Addiction treatment, or rehab, as it is called, is big business. Yet the treatment-center business pales in comparison to the alcohol production, marketing and distribution business. And the resulting tax revenue from alcohol use and treatment for alcohol abuse is immense.

With such huge amounts of money invested in the continuing existence of alcohol use and abuse, is it any wonder that alcohol abuse is not decreasing in North America?

The alcohol production and marketing industry wants to keep the alcohol flowing. The hotel and restaurant industry needs to serve alcohol for economic survival. The alcohol addiction treatment industry is totally dependent on the continuing flow of alcohol. And most of the rest of us enjoy the occasional drink and shrug off the abuse as part of the cost.

Neither alcoholism nor the alcoholism rehab industry is going to shrink any time soon.

Reflection: How much more ready are you now to deal with your life situation than you were when you started reading this book?

Chapter 27
Can Alcoholism be Cured?
Is a Return to Social
Drinking Ever Possible?

The "No-Cure" Camp

Many people, both lay and professional, hold that alcoholism cannot be cured. They argue that once a person is an alcoholic, he will always be an alcoholic, even if he has not had a drink for 30 years.

Within this framework alcoholism is thought of as a progressive disease. It can go into remission, but it cannot be cured.

The implication of this point of view is that if an alcoholic quits drinking permanently, he will still be "in recovery" for the rest of his life.

The no-cure point of view has a wide following.

The "Cure" Camp

There is another school of thought that says alcoholism can be cured. The principal argument in this group is that addiction is a choice. There are good addictions and bad addictions. Work is usually thought of as a good addiction. Alcohol is usually thought of as a bad addiction.

149

Either way, addiction is a choice.

Of those who treat addiction as a choice, some go so far as to say alcoholism is a moral choice. If a person can learn to make better choices—and anyone can—then alcoholism can be cured.

Alcohol Dependence versus Alcohol Abuse

You are probably astute enough to have noticed that in the above discussion of the "cure" and "no-cure" camps, I have been using the word *alcoholism* rather than *alcohol abuse*. This has been quite deliberate.

People on either side of the argument tend to be sloppy about how they define alcoholism.

Strictly speaking, an alcoholic is someone who is dependent upon and addicted to alcohol. This is a small proportion of the people who get into trouble because they abuse alcohol.

There is little evidence that someone who is an advanced alcoholic can successfully move from alcohol addiction to light social drinking. In most cases it seems he cannot. If he starts drinking again the progression to re-dependence is usually fairly rapid.

I speculate that the reason an advanced alcoholic is seldom cured is that by the time he is dependent on alcohol he will be fighting for his very survival. He will be dealing with health issues, social issues, family issues and perhaps legal issues.

An advanced alcoholic will seldom begin to deal with the psychological and spiritual factors that have led to his alcohol abuse and supported him in his addiction. He simply won't ever get around to or choose to deal with his mental health issues, which may be severe.

However, it is still theoretically possible that an advanced alcoholic could choose to change, seek treatment, deal with his mental health problems and eventually reach a point where alcohol was not a part of his identity.

His identity would no longer be stated in terms of whether or not he used or could use alcohol. It would take commitment, time, good luck and probably a lot of money. But if he went the distance and succeeded, it would be a cure.

It would be a cure so long as he didn't drink. The return to addictive drinking levels after relapse tends to be very fast.

It is not clear whether the brain alteration that comes with alcohol abuse ever completely heals. It certainly takes at least a few years.

The Non-Addicted Majority of Alcohol Abusers

Let's turn our attention away from the alcoholic to the much larger group of alcohol abusers who are not yet addicted to alcohol. Here the situation is different. There are two major subgroups.

First are the many who abuse alcohol, but decide to stop abusing alcohol and seek help. They talk to their family doctor. Many go to AA. Some go to treatment centers. Some seek the help of psychologists or other mental health professionals.

The second and much larger group of alcohol abusers is made up of those who don't seek help, but nevertheless permanently stop abusing alcohol.

Their usual pattern while drinking looks like that of any other alcohol abuser. They eventually start bumping into the negative consequences of their drinking. It could be an impaired driving charge. It could be getting fired. It could be a marriage failure. Or they could simply recognize and be tired of the numbing effects of alcohol.

But for whatever reason they decide that their alcohol abuse must stop. And so they cut their consumption to zero or to light social drinking. They simply decide to do it, and then they do it. We all know these people.

For about a year after his wife died, Fred drank very heavily, frequently getting drunk. Now he's back to his old self.

Peter was a very heavy drinker until he had his coronary. Now he drinks only a glass of wine with dinner.

Jim was the town drunk when he was in his twenties. Now is a respected businessman who uses but never abuses alcohol.

The millions of serious alcohol abusers like these simply don't make it into research studies.

Do such people have cravings? Yes. Do they develop tolerance? Yes. Did they sometimes drink uncontrollably? Yes. Did they depend on alcohol to quell their distress? Yes. Those, except for the absence of physical dependence, are the four pillars that define alcoholism.

Were They Cured?

It is interesting that family members, friends, employers and colleagues were probably quite willing to label them as *alcoholics* when they were drinking. Out of kindness their friends may have called them "functioning alcoholics." Certainly any of them would have been welcomed as an alcoholic in recovery at any AA meeting.

But they didn't go for help. They simply cleaned up their acts themselves. What they accomplished was heroic. In certain circles, however, if they were to claim they were cured, they would be met with the demeaning comment that they could not have been alcoholics to start with.

That was my own experience. My alcohol consumption was at the level of the skid-row alcoholic. It was destroying my health. I quit. I spent time and money on dealing with the emotional issues that had led me into alcoholism.

For many years now alcohol has been totally irrelevant to my life. I never crave it. I don't think about it. My drinking or not drinking has not been part of my identity for decades.

However, when I have shared my belief that I have been cured, I have been flatly told that if I wasn't still an alcoholic, I could never have been an alcoholic. What I do know is that I loved my alcohol and I was certainly able to drink under the table most of the confirmed alcoholics I knew at the time. Was I an alcoholic? You be the judge.

As an aside, a similar thing happens any time a person's experience is in conflict with prevailing beliefs. When a friend was diagnosed with ovarian cancer by three cancer specialists, and then declined surgery and proceeded to cure herself energetically, her claim of cure was met with a counterclaim that they must have made a misdiagnosis in the first place.

Such closed-mindedness seems to go hand-in-hand with prevalent beliefs about alcoholism. Your job is to listen, and then take your own counsel.

Conclusion

For the person who has abused alcohol until he has become physically alcohol dependent, there may not be a total cure. But I do not rule out the possibility.

For the alcohol abuser who has not become physically dependent, it is within the realm of possibility for him to stop abusing alcohol and return to light social drinking. Clearly he would have a much greater chance of success if he simply quit drinking. For me the risk of experimenting would be forbiddingly high.

In order to avoid relapse into alcohol abuse, he may require professional help with the underlying mental health issues. But the alcohol abuser who hasn't progressed very far may well be able to stop his problem drinking permanently without outside help. Thousands have.

Reflection: Has your partner quit drinking before, but now drinks more heavily than ever?

Chapter 28
Detoxification Services

Withdrawal Distress

Detoxification services are provided so that people who are using alcohol heavily can have medical supervision while they withdraw from alcohol. The fact is that long-term heavy drinkers may suffer severe emotional and physical distress while ridding their bodies of alcohol and its byproducts.

There may be severe shakes, intense fear, sweating, and even delusions and hallucinations. Sometimes the reactions can be life-threatening.

The reactions to withdrawal can be severe enough that one or another kind of medical intervention is required. Sometimes special medications are used to reduce the severity of the symptoms.

It is difficult to predict who will have the very severe withdrawal symptoms. But it is clear that the longer a person has been drinking and the heavier the drinking the greater their risk of severe withdrawal symptoms.

Unfortunately, unless a person has gone through complete withdrawal recently, there is no real way of knowing whether he will encounter problems.

I recommend putting safey first. If he is a heavy drinker, the safest way to detoxify is under medical supervision.

It is interesting that the presence of severe withdrawal symptoms is one of the criteria for identifying a person as an alcoholic to start with. Yet his reaction to withdrawal cannot be known until he actually attempts it.

Detox Services

Detoxification centers are located in most communities of any size and in many smaller communities throughout North America. If your community doesn't have a detox center, your local hospital will probably have a detoxification protocol. It takes typically from one to four days to withdraw and detoxify.

Detoxification centers are often administratively associated with treatment centers, or at least located nearby. This practice has risen from the fact that treatment centers require a person to be sober to enter their program. A new client may have to use the detoxification service as part of his admittance procedure.

Also, after someone goes through withdrawal and detoxification, he may want to join a treatment program immediately to help him stay sober. He is at highest risk for relapsing during the first few days, weeks and months after withdrawal.

It should be pointed out though that many treatment centers require a period of a few weeks of sobriety prior to admission.

If your partner is a heavy drinker and wants to stop using alcohol completely, and if he won't consider a detoxification center or a hospital, at the very least, discuss the situation with his family doctor. You may be able to supervise his withdrawal, but have medical assistance on call in case of emergency.

Although less common, the former heavy drinker may go through detoxification symptom-free, as a quirk of genetics, it turns out. That was my own experience. The problem is that this is hard or impossible to predict. And it is not worth taking a chance on.

Reflection: Do you know how difficult detoxification would be for your partner? Ask him how difficult he thinks it would be.

Chapter 29
An Introduction to
Alcoholics Anonymous

Alcoholics Anonymous, commonly known as AA, is a voluntary organization of men and women who believe they have an alcohol problem. AA exists so that people with alcohol abuse problems can help one another by sharing their experience, hopes and triumphs. Although AA has no formal treatment programs, AA has been an important factor in the personal healing and growth of large numbers of people.

AA has chapters in most communities, but it has no bureaucratic superstructure. There are no fees. Hundreds of thousands of people seek help through AA every year. Nevertheless it is estimated that only four percent of the problem drinkers in North America ever get to an AA meeting.

AA Has Been a Lifesaver

AA has helped multitudes of people with alcohol problems. I have personally known many, both inside and outside of my practice. Several of my own children have received help through AA to get their lives back on track. I have friends who probably would be dead by now, were it not for the help they received through AA.

AA has been a lifesaver to many and will continue to be the salvation of multitudes of problem drinkers.

In any community there may be AA meetings going on regularly and frequently. In fact, on a daily basis there may be several meetings to choose from, should support be needed immediately.

Besides the public AA groups, there are private AA groups that we don't hear about. For example a community may have a non-advertised AA group strictly for healthcare professionals.

Any of these groups may provide invaluable support to someone with a desire to quit drinking, or to a former alcohol abuser who is in the early stages of recovery.

The first year of sobriety is the highest risk period for most former alcoholics. It is the time when they are most vulnerable to returning to their alcohol abuse. And the first six months are the worst part of that first year. Of the first six months the first thirty days are critical for those who have quit drinking. This is the time they need maximum support.

For many former alcohol abusers AA is a lifesaver during their first year or more of sobriety.

Thank You to the Lifers

Some recovering alcoholics continue to attend AA meetings for the rest of their lives—twenty years, thirty years, and more. Some do it in part because they have accepted the assumption that if they don't stay with AA they will sink back into practicing alcoholism and die. It could well be true for some of them, particularly if they were well entrenched in their addiction.

Other former alcohol abusers hold a somewhat different view. They realize they are probably past the risk of relapsing and dying from alcoholism, but they find AA instrumental in their own personal healing and growth. AA helps them deepen their consciousness of life. AA becomes the venue of their psychological and spiritual growth.

Not only do they stay with AA to continue their own growth, but they stay to offer help to others on their individual paths to sobriety. They want to give back. They become sponsors of the newer, more fragile members. They speak at meetings and rallies. Lifelong bonds of friendship are built within AA.

The long-term AA adherents, in my opinion, are the people who have given continuity to the AA movement. We have a lot to thank them for.

A Short-term Affair

For most recovering alcohol abusers, however, AA is a short-term affair. The exact numbers are not known, but one study suggested that nineteen out of twenty people who attend an AA meeting will not be attending AA meetings a year later.

What happened to them? Some did, of course, continue in their alcoholism. Others got the boost they needed from AA, cleaned up their lives and moved on. A couple of my own children have done this.

Yet others reacted negatively to some of the *doctrine* they perceived within AA and left without getting as much help as they might have had they stayed.

When a person goes to AA meetings, he is encouraged to admit that his life has "become unmanageable" and he is "powerless over alcohol." Perhaps this was too hard to take and he protested he was not powerless over alcohol. Then someone with the best of intentions drove him away by telling him he was "in denial."

Remember, AA is a lay organization.

Spiritual versus Religious

Early on in a person's association with AA, he is encouraged to turn his life over to his *"higher power, or to God, whatever he conceives Him to be."* This "higher power" can sound too much like the Christian God for someone who is atheist, or Hindu, or aboriginal.

AA claims to be *spiritual, but nonreligious.* Is AA religious? The American appeals courts say so. Rulings have been that AA is religious, specifically Christian. Critics have referred to AA as a Christian cult that forces people to pray, and coerces them to accept a Christian-type God or accept that the alternative is to die from their alcoholism.

From a quick look at the beginnings of AA, the roots of the Christian bias are obvious. Originally AA focused on alcoholic derelicts who were dying from their alcoholism. The times were decidedly not multicultural, at least in the United States. The surrounding culture was solidly Christian.

The skid-row alcoholics that AA reached probably were powerless over alcohol. If they relapsed into drinking, they would likely die of alcoholism-related maladies.

The founders of AA believed that what a derelict alcoholic needed was a "religious experience." It made sense to appeal to the alcoholic's Christian roots. The method worked, and lives were saved.

They called the organization *spiritual* because they didn't want it to be aligned with any particular Christian denomination.

Over the years there has been a gradual recognition that the notion of spirituality goes far beyond Christian religions. In my opinion spirituality broadly defined is still of critical importance to the AA movement. When people are seeking to transform their lives, they are engaged in a decidedly spiritual endeavor.

Unfortunately, there is always a lag in shifting language and attitude. AA is a broadly-based volunteer association. No one tells an individual chapter to change. This tends to make for slow progress. However, it can be a blessing in disguise. It means there is great variation among the different chapters. With a bit of searching, a problem drinker can usually find a group that works for him.

Summary

Let me sum up. AA has helped and continues to help millions of people in their transition from severe alcohol abuse to sobriety. But there are also people in need who find it difficult to receive help from AA, because of perceived pressure to accept Christian doctrine and the powerlessness-over-alcohol doctrine.

Others cannot go to AA because they believe it is absolutely essential to their personal and professional lives that their alcohol problems remain private.

A further minority has an aversion to saying anything in a group context—extreme shyness, extreme shame, fear of public speaking, paranoia, etc.

AA has been instrumental in helping millions of people with problem drinking. However, AA is only one route, albeit a major one, a person may take to get non-professional help with overcoming problem drinking.

The next chapter deals with the 12-step program.

Reflection: How would someone use AA meetings as an instrument of personal growth?

Chapter 30
Alcoholics Anonymous
Twelve-Step Program

If you are ever around AA circles, you will hear people talk about "*the program*." The reference is to the Twelve Step program of AA. Knowing something about the Twelve Step program is essential to understanding the success of AA. It is also important to your understanding of a subsequent chapter on treatment centers.

The founders of AA believed that recovery from alcoholism was greatly facilitated through some sort of religious or spiritual experience. That notion is very much reflected in the principles that were developed within AA.

The Twelve Step program is a series of stages that AA encourages recovering alcoholics to go through in order to be whole again and in order to stay sober. When you hear a former alcohol abuser say "I'm working my program," what he is saying is that he is working through the Twelve Step program for recovery.

The Twelve-Steps

Alcoholics Anonymous, the "Big Book" of AA, was first published in 1939. The twelve steps were elaborated and updated in the 1952 book, **Twelve Steps and Twelve Traditions**. (The twelve traditions are about how AA operates as an organization.)

The Twelve Steps are a group of spiritual principles which recovering alcoholics are encouraged to adopt as a way of life on their way to being happy and whole.

Step 1 is the admission of powerlessness over alcohol.

Other steps involve belief in a higher power, doing a "moral inventory," admitting wrongdoing, making amends and continuing with personal growth.

Clearly, if someone were to work through the twelve steps, his life would be transformed.

"We Were Powerless over Alcohol"

It should be remembered that when someone first goes to AA, he is usually in a vulnerable, fragile state. He may feel he's a victim of alcohol. However, it could well be that his alcohol abuse is secondary to some other trauma he hasn't yet faced, and he may not be alcohol dependent.

Many people who go to AA are in fact powerless over alcohol. Others, however, have an alcohol abuse problem that they will overcome when they identify and deal with the underlying mental health issues; they are simply seeking help from AA.

I suggest that it is in the client's best interest to build on whatever strength and sense of power he has as he attempts to deal with his alcohol problem.

Many women who have an alcohol abuse problem already have all too much life experience with lacking power. I am not alone in contending it is generally not in a woman's best interest to further emphasize her powerlessness. Rather, her most productive healing will come through building up a sense of personal power and personal responsibility.

AA groups vary a lot from one to another. If your partner has an alcohol problem and finds a particular AA group to be unhelpful because it is antagonistic to his personal beliefs, he should simply find another, more compatible group. Not finding a compatible AA group on the first try is insufficient reason for giving up on AA.

Reflection: Has your partner ever mentioned AA. Has he ever attended a meeting? Assuming he hasn't been to a meeting, how do you think he would respond to it?

Chapter 31
Are There Alternatives to the AA Twelve Step Program?

What a lot of people do not recognize is that there are numerous alternatives to the AA Twelve Step program. Especially if you live in a larger city, you may find other groups who have regular support meetings and welcome anyone who thinks they may have a problem with drinking. Furthermore, a number of them have online meetings for those who can't get to a regular meeting.

Clearly, AA does not suit everyone, even if it is the only show in town. Many people who would like to overcome their alcohol abuse are put off by AA, especially by its perceived religious nature, its emphasis on being powerless and its underlying notion of alcoholism as a disease.

If you are trying to educate yourself about alcohol and drug treatment options, this chapter is mandatory reading. Website references are given for each option.

A couple of the options have been designed specifically for women. If you are searching for treatment options for your partner, take a look at these options anyway. Sometimes there is an offshoot organization for men. In all cases the principles are important.

Women for Sobriety (WFS)

Women for Sobriety was founded in the mid-seventies, specifically to help women with alcohol abuse problems. It came out of recognition that the psychological needs of women in recovery from alcoholism were different from those of men.

Following the initial success of WFS, they had many requests from men for the same kind of help. So **Men for Sobriety (MFS)** came about. You can find out about MFS at the WFS web address www.womenforsobriety.org.

As an organization WFS provides self-help materials for women dealing with alcoholism, and it helps women to establish small self-help groups in their own communities. These groups operate under a set of simple and empowering principles.

Their thirteen empowering principles are what make **Women for Sobriety** exciting to me. Their "New Life" acceptance program includes a simple acknowledment of the drinking problem, a recognition of how our thoughts can empower us, and an acceptance of the importance of love and happiness.

Compared to the AA twelve steps, the principles are empowering and positive.

There are now WFS chapters in many communities around the world. If you have an alcohol problem yourself and are looking for help, take a look at WFS. Check out their website at www.womenforsobriety.org.

When you contact them, they can tell you whether or not there is a WFS chapter in your community. If there isn't, they can show you how to start one.

There is a lot more to WFS and MFS. But if you are just beginning to explore sources of help for your partner, or you are at the stage of even thinking about getting help for yourself, your search would be incomplete without checking out **Women for Sobriety**.

SMART Recovery

"SMART" refers to Self-Management and Recovery Training. SMART Recovery begins with the premise that alcohol addiction is a bad habit, not a disease. Since it is not a disease, there are no labels.

It works from four points based in research:

1. Enhancing and Maintaining Motivation to Abstain

2. Coping with Urges

3. Problem Solving (Managing thoughts, feelings and behaviors)

4. Lifestyle Balance (Balancing momentary and enduring satisfactions)

Lifestyle balance is the goal. SMART provides a number of online tools to help people get there. Although there are SMART Recovery mutual support face-to-face meetings in numerous communities, they offer quite a number of online meetings as well.

SMART Recovery is definitely an alternative worth checking out at www.smartrecovery.org/intro/.

LifeRing

LifeRing also offers mutual-help meetings. It emphasizes sobriety, but without laying on guilt or shame for drinking.

It takes the position that spiritual/religious issues are a person's own business, so there is no talk of a "higher power." They don't pray at meetings.

LifeRing is the ultimate self-help approach, because they do not buy into the notion of a single path. Each person must experiment to find the approaches that work for him. There is no program and no dogma.

LifeRing has a number of online support options at www.unhooked.com.

16 Steps for Discovery and Empowerment

This program was developed by Dr. Charlotte Kasl. Her sixteen steps were developed partly in reaction to the fact that the AA principles were written over sixty years ago by white Christian men for white Christian alcoholic men. Such beginnings have left many people out, especially women.

Dr. Kasl has sought to deal with the whole person—social, mental, physical, and spiritual. She developed her sixteen-step program specifically for women, although her principles are universally applicable.

The sixteen steps are spelled out on her website, www.charlottekasl.com, which clearly presents an underlying philosophy of empowerment, authenticity, personal wisdom and taking responsibility for one's own life and life circumstances.

Dr. Kasl's work should be considered an essential part of your education about recovery from addiction.

Save Our Selves (SOS)

SOS welcomes anyone interested in sobriety. It furthers the idea that recovery is easier and more effective if supported by others who are going through the same struggle. In this way it is like AA. Unlike AA, however, it does not limit itself to one theory of recovery from addiction. Any path will do if it works for you.

Again, there are self-help groups in the US and other countries. Whether or not your partner will participate in an SOS group, the SOS website is worth reviewing at

www.secularsobriety.org.

Be sure to take a look at the SOS toolkit at

www.secularsobriety.org/toolkit.html.

Moderation Management (MM)

Most of the self-help groups for problem drinkers are aimed at their members' maintaining sobriety. However, as I have said elsewhere, the evidence is clear that many people who presently abuse alcohol can clean up their acts to return to responsible moderate drinking.

MM maintains that ninety percent of today's problem drinkers actively avoid the traditional programs based on a goal of abstinence. **MM** has found that programs are more successful if they give people a choice of abstinence or moderation.

MM encourages people to take responsibility for whatever choice they make about their own recovery. Their approach places value on people helping other people as part of their own recovery. They emphasize self esteem, self management, and treating one another with dignity and respect.

Their meetings are based on their "Nine Steps Toward Moderation and Positive Lifestyle Changes," which you can read on their website. There is a lot of other very practical information on the **MM** web site www.moderation.org.

A Final Note on Alternatives to AA

Having outlined various alternatives to AA, I need to add a caution. Your partner's determination to conquer his alcoholism, heal from its emotional causes and change his lifestyle so that alcohol is no longer part of his life is far more important than where he goes for support. If he is highly motivated, any approach will help. If he is attending meetings under duress, nothing may help. It's up to him.

If the only local support group is AA and he wants to succeed in his recovery, he can benefit from AA even if his beliefs may conflict with what he thinks he hears there. What he has in common with all the others is they are all attempting to recover from an alcoholic lifestyle.

Reflection: Knowing what you know now, how do you think you would handle a comment from your partner that went something like the following? "I'd like to quit, but I will never go to AA."

Chapter 32
Alcohol and Drug Addiction Rehab Centers

Any industry serving two million high-paying clients a month (in the US alone) is big business. The creation, marketing and management of alcohol and drug addiction treatment centers are big business. Note that the popular term "rehab center" is just another term for "treatment center."

Most problem drinkers share a need for immediate gratification. As a group they tend to be short on patience. As AA groups became widespread in the United States, they attracted large numbers of problem drinkers who wanted help quickly.

But AA itself is a non-professional fellowship; it is not a treatment program. By its own constitution it cannot charge for services.

The Emergence of Addiction Treatment Centers

With the early growth of AA and its members' demand for rehab, treatment centers began to appear. Before long thousands of treatment centers had been created to satisfy the urgency unintentionally created by AA.

And how did they staff them? In many cases it was the very people who, through AA, were in recovery from their alcohol abuse and were now helping others through AA. These recovering alcoholics got some training and began establishing treatment centers and working as counselling staff.

Given the historical relationship between AA and the treatment centers, it is not surprising that most of the treatment centers, at least in North America, are based on the AA model of recovery and on its Twelve Step program.

The need for treatment, of course, was there before the creation of treatment centers. But AA became an excellent recruiting agency for such centers. Alcoholics' need for treatment was preached until it became a part of the public perception.

And the new treatment centers quietly recruited staff. AA continues to supply treatment centers with clients, and indirectly with staff.

The approach was called the Minnesota Model, a huge improvement over the mental hospitals or jails of the 1940s. It is based on the assumptions that alcoholism is not just a symptom of something else, but a primary disease, and that mental, spiritual and physical components must be addressed to achieve the goal of lifetime abstinence

The Failure to Deal with Mental Health Issues

Many treatment centers are owned and administered by people who do not comprehend the pervasiveness of mental health problems that accompany the addiction. Consequently, they have not seen the need for top mental health professionals on their staffs.

Of course, the industry does include some very highly trained mental health professionals. Even though these mental health experts are doing their best and their numbers are growing, we still have to acknowledge the general under-training of treatment center staff in mental health counseling. Given the real presence of mental health problems in their clientele, there exists a significant deficiency in many treatment centers.

The Absence of Other Specialists

Treatment centers often do not have the relevant medical specialists on call. They do not have available expertise in the nutritional treatment of addiction. They typically do not have an association with a chiropractor, acupuncturist or massage therapist.

This absence of a range of expertise is a reflection of the treatment model. The Minnesota model emphasizes managing addictive behavior rather than curing it, since its underlying assumption is that alcoholism cannot be cured. It follows that treatment centers based on the model would not have cure as a goal, and therefore would have no reason to retain all these expensive specialists.

A few years ago a piece of research was conducted at one of the more prestigious treatment centers in the United States to see what effect a particular chiropractic manipulation (torque release technique) would have on their client retention rate. The finding was that all the residents who received regular torque release chiropractic treatment as part of their addiction treatment completed the program. Normally, about thirty percent of clients complete that particular program.[8]

The underlying scientific basis of such a striking finding is not clear. More research will be necessary. I predict that further experimentation with chiropractic and also with acupuncture will show both to be important adjuncts to the treatment programs which are now the norm.

Recommendation

A little over ten percent of the treatment centers in the United States de-emphasize the AA model. These tend on average to be more oriented towards cure, and consequently, they tend to have more varied staff.

I use the word "de-emphasize" deliberately. As our understanding of treatment methods grows and the rehab industry evolves, the underlying model is becoming less important as a factor in choosing a treatment center.

This minority of treatment centers appeals to a small but growing segment of society that is less willing to accept conventional wisdom like "Alcoholism is a disease," "Alcoholism cannot be cured," or "Alcoholism is genetic," but still recognizes the value of a residential addiction treatment program. Having said that, however, it should be noted that rehab programs based on the Minnesota model vary widely regarding how rigidly they adhere to the conventional wisdom.

If you are looking for a treatment center for your functioning alcoholic partner, my advice is to do your research and be selective. If he will be going into a treatment center for thirty to sixty days at a cost of $350-$500 or more a day, it really doesn't matter where the treatment center is located: the cost of getting there and back is minor compared to the cost of being there. So choose the best.

Some treatment centers have excellent family programs, usually an intensive weekend of support for the family of the client in the program. Your participation in a family program is the one advantage to choosing a treatment center in your own or a nearby region. It would be ideal if the best treatment center for your partner also has a family program and is located in your region.

Mandatory Treatment

In the United States many people are court mandated to attend a treatment center and AA. For example, a traffic accident involving alcohol often concludes with a court order for rehab and AA.

No one asks whether the offender is addicted to alcohol. What is known is only that he abused alcohol and got in an accident.

I have seen estimates that in the United States as many as half of the clients of alcohol and drug treatment centers are there because the court ordered them to be there or because an employer required them to be there as a condition of their continued employment.

If your partner attends a treatment center involuntarily, his chances of successful completion of the program and continued sobriety are poor. The odds of success are even lower if a lot of the other residents are also there under duress.

His chances of long-term success are greatly increased if he really wants to change his alcohol-supported lifestyle and is open and willing to do whatever it takes to overcome his addiction and live a healthier lifestyle. Success is even more achievable when everyone else in the program is motivated to change. That way they can work as a team.

Benefits and Drawbacks of a Treatment Center Program

The group setting provides a major benefit. Many if not all long-term alcohol abusers have underdeveloped social skills, regardless of their socioeconomic status. Recognizing this, treatment centers work with clients in helping them gain social skills to be able to live with and interact with other people. The group setting of the treatment center is ideal for their clients' development of basic social skills and related life skills.

But there is an even more important benefit from being in a group setting. The clients who are nearer to their 6-week graduation date have already made huge progress in changing their lives. Beginning clients are entering an already established, cohesive peer support group. The positive influence on the new people of peer support, peer teaching and peer coaching and bonding cannot be overemphasized.

During the first three weeks of rehab most clients experience an increase in self esteem and confidence, sometimes a dramatic increase. Buoyed by these good feelings and a few weeks of sobriety, some will want to drop out of treatment, really believing they don't need it anymore: they believe they can handle things on their own. And addicts tend to be impatient.

It would be a big mistake to withdraw. Leaving any treatment program prematurely increases the risk of failure. At three weeks they may have taken in the basics of addiction recovery, but they are at the very beginning stages of lifestyle readjustment. Recovery is a long-term process. Fortunately, the peer group can be an important role in encouraging them to stay.

For some people the potential loss of privacy is a major drawback of attending a treatment center. Public figures are particularly vulnerable. If their problem drinking were to become public, it could damage their careers. However, given the recent numbers of high-profile people who attend rehab, the stigma seems to be lessening.

Reflection: If your partner decides he needs help in changing his life, what roadblocks to his enrolling in a 6-week residential treatment program would you anticipate?

Chapter 33
Would an Individualized Therapeutic Program Be a Better Option for Him?

If you are looking for serious help for your functioning alcoholic partner, you might not even think of one excellent option, an individualized program with a professional. You realize that your partner will probably require quite a bit of help. It is unlikely that you would immediately think of an option which involves paying a professional $150 to $250 per hour for as long as it takes.

I am not speaking of his having a few sessions with an alcohol and drug counselor in a free community clinic. A problem drinker can end up feeling like a ping-pong ball between mental health and addiction services.

Rather, I am speaking of going to a psychologist or other professional who is expert in treating both mental health problems and addiction problems. I would further recommend that the professional have training and experience in the use of the new energy psychology therapies. Healing can take place without energy psychology, but it may take longer.

Furthermore, if the individual program is to be truly successful, the psychologist will have a collaborative relationship with other service providers—a medical doctor, a naturopathic physician, a chiropractor, a massage therapist, an acupuncturist and a nutritionist. He or she may also be able to call on a minister, priest, rabbi or other religious counselor if appropriate. A detox center will also be available if needed.

Is Your Partner Prepared to Do Whatever It Takes?

If you and your partner choose for him the individualized therapeutic program option, he should plan on meeting once or twice or even three times per week, with homework in between sessions, for an extended period of time. Plan on doing the recommended extras, like seeing the naturopath and the chiropractor, joining a physical exercise program (with a coach if possible), having medical checkups, and getting nutrition counseling if advised.

He will attend the AA or other peer support groups. He could benefit from joining a men's group or doing volunteer work in a group setting.

Be prepared for the need for relationship counseling and coaching as part of the program, especially in the later phases.

The work may be quite intense for a few months, and it may need to continue at a less intense level for significantly longer. Just how long depends on the level of alcohol dependence your partner had reached and the extent of his underlying mental health problems. It will take several years for his brain to fully recover from severe alcoholism.

The period of post-acute withdrawal is popularly called the "dry drunk" phase. He may need periodic professional help during this period.

In short, if you and your partner are seeking an individualized program, he should be prepared to do whatever it takes to succeed with the program. To do less than that could prove to be a disappointing and costly failure.

Of course, the same comment applies to his going to a treatment center. Many people attend treatment center programs a number of times before they have overcome their alcohol problem. Similarly, if you embark on an individualized program, there could be one or more false starts.

Not a Cheap Alternative

It would not be wise to look at the individualized program as a cheaper alternative to a treatment center program. He will be pursuing an individually structured path more focused on him. If you are thinking of spending $15,000 on a treatment center program, budget the same for the individual work. You will probably end up spending less and it will be spread over a much longer period, but both of you should be prepared to do whatever it takes.

Again, if he could go away to a treatment center for couple of months, he could also go anywhere for the individual therapy. If he opts for treatment at a distant location, relationship counseling on his return ought to be arranged in advance of his going away for treatment. Similarly, extended periodic counseling during the post-acute withdrawal phase should be arranged.

If you can find a professional able to structure a good individual program nearby, your partner could live at home. However, the home dynamics may complicate the treatment. So there is a trade-off.

Benefits and Drawbacks of an Individualized Program

If the person with the drinking problem—whether he is alcohol dependent or not—has well developed social skills and has a high profile in his community, he will value his privacy. For him the individualized program may be a good option. It assures privacy, can fit into his busy lifestyle without major disruption and can be offered over an extended period of time.

As with the treatment center programs, the biggest risk of failure is from dropping out prematurely. It's easier to drop out of an individualized program because there is usually no payment in advance, and this could be a drawback. For the individualized program to work, the client needs to take it just as seriously as he would if he had paid $15,000 in advance.

Completing any major program is a big commitment. Does your partner have the staying power to follow through?

Reflection: What would work better for your partner, a residential treatment program or an outpatient individualized program?

Action: Draw a line down the middle of a page in your notebook, and write "Residential Rehab" at the top of one column and "Individualized Outpatient Program" at the top of the other column. Then, thinking of your partner specifically, list the benefits and advantages under each approach.

Chapter 34
Do Your Research and
Find the Appropriate Rehab

Seven Major Recommendations

A number of recommendations are implicit in the preceding chapters. In this chapter I will make them explicit.

The seven major recommendations listed below apply to any form of rehab or treatment for alcohol abuse problems. It doesn't matter whether you are looking at an individualized program or a treatment center program. Each of the seven recommendations is generic; that is, it applies to anyone seeking treatment for alcohol abuse or alcohol addiction. The seven recommendations also apply when seeking treatment for a drug addiction problem.

However, the theme of **Living with a Functioning Alcoholic** is that of helping you, a woman whose partner has a drinking problem. Therefore, each recommendation is stated in terms of helping you guide your partner when he has expressed interest in quitting drinking and rebuilding his life.

1.   **Whatever program you seek should be built on your partner's strengths.** For example, if he believes he can beat his alcohol problem, but would like some help in doing so, his self-confidence should be honored and built upon.

2.   **Your partner should never be told or urged to believe he is a victim.** Being a victim is a mentally unhealthy place to be. Getting out of the victim mentality and taking responsibility is very important to his overcoming his alcohol problem. It is also important to his emotional and spiritual health and growth.

3.   **Examine the credentials and breadth of expertise the treatment team offers.** What additional therapeutic service does the treatment center offer? How strong is the mental health component? Look for breadth as well as depth. If you are considering an individualized program, ask what other professionals and services the psychologist has access to.

4.   **Look for some level of expertise in energy psychology within the team.** Not everyone will agree with this. I believe it is an indicator of the level of openness of the program managers to innovation and new cutting-edge technology.

5.   **Question the ethical boundaries of treatment**, whether you are looking at an individualized program or a treatment center program. For example, are people required to pray even if they don't believe in it? Are people treated with respect and dignity? Are personal boundaries honored? Are confidences kept?

6. **Check references if possible**. I say "if possible," because the names of clients will be confidential unless they have given written permission to use their names. You may have to be creative in getting opinions as to how good a treatment center or therapist is.

7. **Trust your instincts as you are evaluating options.** If something sounds too good to be true, it probably is. If you have nagging reservations about a particular option, look further. The last thing either of you need is for him to experience another failure.

Reflection: What personal work will you need to do to get to a place where you can "trust your insticts" in life with a functioning alcoholic partner?

Postscript

The underlying message of this book is one of hope. No matter how bad things have become, you have the power not only to survive, but to thrive. And no matter how stuck in his alcoholism your partner is, he can get out of that stuck place if he truly wants to. If he doesn't want to, you need to prepare yourself to make some choices.

Furthermore, having read the book, you should have a better perspective on addiction, knowledge of some new self-help tools and a better understanding of how to help your partner if he wants to change. He may need professional help to stop drinking and transform the underlying issues, but good help is available.

You have my very best wishes for recovery and transformation. May your life be one of happiness and fulfillment!

Further Education

If you have not already done so, go to www.neillneill.com, and leave your first name and email address so you can

1. Download my report, **"Personal Change Manifesto."**

2. Receive future updates, articles, notices of tele-seminars, courses, recordings and things I have not even thought of yet.

If you are interested in teleseminars or workshops, contact me at DrNeill@neillneill.com, and if possible let me know what topic or topics would most interest you. Call me if you would like to discuss. I am also available as a speaker.

My new website, www.alcoholism.neillneill.com, is now open. It covers practical subjects related to alcoholism and addiction. There will be ongoing publication of articles that would be of interest to anyone living in the presence of addiction. So, join my email notification list at www.alcoholism.neillneill.com.
Tell me what you want me to write about.

Dr. Neill Neill
235 Crescent Road West
Qualicum Beach
British Columbia
Canada V9K 1J9
(250) 752-8684
DrNeill@neillneill.com
www.neillneill.com
www.alcoholism.neillneill.com

About Dr. Neill

Dr. Neill obtained his Ph. D. in psychology in 1968 from the University of Western Ontario with a grant from the Addiction Research Foundation of Ontario. His career has spanned mental health and addictions work, as well as university teaching and business.

He lives with his wife Eileen in Qualicum Beach on Vancouver Island, British Columbia, Canada. He divides his time among his writing, his private practice in psychological counseling and life coaching, and his work as consulting psychologist for the Sunshine Coast Health Centre, a private drug and alcohol treatment center for men.

Prior to establishing his private practice, his lifelong interest and background in trauma counseling led him to be the psychologist for a remote northern Indian village and their Alcohol and Drug Treatment Center.

Many of the people he sees in his practice have addictions or are living with someone with an addiction. He helps his clients build on their strengths and create for themselves a brightness of the future.

Dr. Neill, Diplomate-Comprehensive Energy Psychology, applies some of the new energy therapies in helping people heal and grow. He speaks and writes of energy psychology as cutting-edge psycho-technology.

Dr. Neill writes two very popular newspaper columns, one with the byline, *Hope and Happiness*. He is a regular contributor to Synergy Magazine. He frequently publishes new articles under the banner **Practical Psychology for Capable People** on his website www.NeillNeill.com. He may be contacted at DrNeill@neillneill.com.

Appendix A
Alcoholism Test

The *Alcoholism Test* is designed for anyone who suspects their partner is a functioning alcoholic. It is aimed, not at the partner with the drinking problem, but at you who cares for him.

1. Your husband sometimes admits he has a drinking problem. He quipped about being a functioning alcoholic.

Dr. Neill: If he sometimes thinks he has a drinking problem, he probably has. Intuition is usually right. See Chapter 4.

2. He has sought help for his drinking at least once that you know of. He may have even joked about going to an alcohol addiction treatment center. He has sought professional help for emotional problems where drinking was probably part of the problem. He has attended an AA meeting. He has tried to quit more than once.

Dr. Neill: If he has gone beyond talk and has sought help or tried to quit, he knows he has a problem. The extent of the problem is the big question. See Chapter 4.

3. You sometimes think he has a drinking problem. You have asked someone for advice about his drinking.

Dr. Neill: Your intuition about the drinking may be dead on, just like his. Pay attention, but don't jump to conclusions just yet. See Chapter 4.

4. He comes from an alcoholic family.

Dr. Neill: Growing up in an alcoholic environment does a lot of emotional damage. Some children grow up to be total abstainers; others become drinkers. Alcohol helps to mask the memories of abuse. However, sometimes using only a little bit of alcohol can bring up such fearful memories that he thinks he is becoming an alcoholic. So just because someone comes from an alcoholic family, it doesn't mean he has an alcohol problem. See Chatper 18.

5. He often has a drink in the morning. Sometimes you find him drinking by himself. He sometimes gets drunk without meaning to. He sometimes can't remember what he did or said during the previous evening of drinking.

Dr. Neill: These are very tell-tale signs of alcoholism. The first three statements suggest that drinking has become a compulsion. That is to say, there is a loss of control, and that is suggestive of addictive drinking. The last item describes alcoholic blackout, again characteristic of longer-term alcohol abuse. See Chapters 4 and 7.

6. He has sometimes denied drinking when he obviously was drinking. You know that he hides alcohol so others won't see it. He gets resentful, defensive and angry if anyone comments on his drinking.

Dr. Neill: Denial is the major line of defense for most problem drinkers. The reality of his alcoholism is not changed by his denial. See Chapters 11, 17 and 21.

7. Your husband has lost days at work or school because of drinking. He has gotten into fights when drinking. He has lost friends over his drinking. There has been a charge of driving under the influence.

Dr. Neill: These and many other negative things begin to happen when the drinking has become a compulsion. Often there are accompanying financial and marital strains. Judgment deteriorates. What counts is not the individual incident, but whether there is a pattern of such events. See Chapter 5.

8. He says he needs alcohol to reduce tension or stress, and a drink helps him build his self-confidence.

Dr. Neill: Many high-functioning alcoholics have low self-esteem. Perhaps most do. The real issue is whether or not your husband has become dependent on the alcohol to overcome another mental health problem, low self-esteem. See Chapters 6 and 14.

9. He has accused you or others of "making him drink." He drinks more heavily after a quarrel. He sometimes becomes verbally or physically abusive when drinking.

Dr. Neill: Blaming others or justifying his behavior, rather than taking responsibility, is a common emotional problem in relationships, but it can be especially exaggerated in alcoholic families. If his drinking is accompanied by abuse, verbal or physical, you are not in a safe place. Take it seriously. See Chapter 24.

10. You often worry about his drinking and lose sleep over it. You feel responsible for his actions. You make threats that you don't follow through on. You get him to make promises he will likely break. You sometimes make excuses for him or cover for him when he has been drinking.

Dr. Neill: These behaviors on your part strongly suggest you have entered into the "alcoholic dance." Your partner may well be a functioning alcoholic, but you have become codependent. All of these behaviors, no matter how well-intentioned, do more to support his alcoholism than to remedy it. See Chapter 16.

11. You feel alone, fearful and anxious a lot of the time. You are beginning to lose self-respect and hate yourself. You sometimes question your own sanity.

Dr. Neill: These are the normal mental health consequences of staying a long time in a codependent relationship, with or without alcohol abuse. Codependence helps no one. As long as you are safe from violence, you may not need to leave the relationship to break out of the codependence. You may be able to break the cycle of codependence with self-help strategies, but you could need professional help. See Chapters 22 and 23.

Final Thoughts

As I hope you have concluded from going through this exercise, understanding whether or not your partner is an alcoholic is not simply a matter of counting drinks or counting answers to a questionnaire. The issue is quite complex. My hope is, however, that the exercise has helped you to see more clearly what you are dealing with.